My Angel Without Wings

My Angel Without Wings

Lucy Perillo Buttermark

TATE PUBLISHING
AND ENTERPRISES, LLC

Published by Tate Publishing & Enterprises, LLC
127 E. Trade Center Terrace | Mustang, Oklahoma 73064 USA
1.888.361.9473 | www.tatepublishing.com

Tate Publishing is committed to excellence in the publishing industry. The company reflects the philosophy established by the founders, based on Psalm 68:11,
"The Lord gave the word and great was the company of those who published it."

Book design copyright © 2013 by Tate Publishing, LLC. All rights reserved.
Cover artwork by: Gregory Perillo
Cover design by Allen Jomoc
Interior design by Jomar Ouano

Published in the United States of America

ISBN: 978-1-62510-979-8
1. Biography & Autobiography / Personal Memoir
2. Family & Relationships / Children With Special Needs
13.02.14

Cover Artwork by

Gregory Perillo.

World renowned artist and sculptor.

Dedication

I would like to dedicate this book to my husband, John, who was there for me every step of the way and helped me with Johnny-Boy as he grew up.

Contents

Chapter 1

My Three Loves

Nothing is impossible if you really want it, as long as it is something good.

My father, Gregorio Perillo

Before I met my husband, my first love was my father. Thanks to him, though we lived during the Great Depression, we were rich in three distinct ways. First, we were rich in style. My father was a tailor and designer, so he fashioned all our school clothes for my three siblings and me. "You will be the best-dressed kids in school," he bragged. And we were.

Second, we were rich in patriotism. My father deeply loved America, even though my parents were Italian immigrants and new to Staten Island. One day, we were all getting ready for school. "What are you doing, Father?" I had asked.

"I am going to school. I will learn English." He straightened his tie with an enthusiasm that made us excited to study too. As he learned English, he studied and practiced with such dedication that you'd think he was being paid a million dollars to do it. It's no wonder that he eventually spoke four different languages. He was a true self-starter and self-learned in everything. "Everyone in my household will speak English at all times," he insisted as his skills grew. We looked at our mother, who rolled her eyes and muttered in Italian.

Last, we were rich in love. And *I* was the richest. As the youngest child, I was closest to my father. My oldest brother was fifteen years my elder, so I was like an only child. My brothers were making their way in the art world, and my sister was raising a family. Father always tended to our large garden, lush with fresh fruits and vegetables. I eyed the apples, so plump that they were threatening. "They are the size of your head, Lucy." My father winked. "You could kill someone with these things."

Every morning it was my job to march to the hen house and gather eggs from the coup. If I ever saw my father on the way there, he would tousle my hair. We were poor but always had something to eat, were comfortable, and got by. I thank my father for that. Seeing others' situations, I never complained when doing my chores.

As I grew older, I knew the courage it took to emigrate from one's homeland to start anew in New York. But my parents not only survived, they thrived. My father's upbeat attitude instilled confidence not only in him but also in myself for years to come. "Nothing is impossible if you really want it, as long as it is something good," he always told me.

I met my next love, my husband-to-be, John Buttermark, when we both attended Curtis High School. We locked eyes at a dance at P.S. 29. His eyes reminded me of deep blue oceans. We were statuesque in admiration. I straightened my chocolate curls, hoping no hair was astray. It was love at first sight, and I knew that he was the man I was going to marry. I was only fifteen years old at the time. I brought him home to meet my family, and they all loved him. Father especially approved, which made me happy because his opinion was the most important. "That John Buttermark is a good man," my father would say.

John and I were married when I was eighteen years old.

"Let's go grab our American dream," John said, squeezing my hand after our wedding ceremony. The world was our oyster: we wanted to find jobs, save up

for a house, and have children. I got a job at Dunn &
Bradstreet in Manhattan and saved all of my salary for a
down payment on our own house. We then lived on my
husband's salary. Finally, we had enough money to buy a
house, and I soon became pregnant.

On a rainy morning on April 30, 1961, John
Buttermark Jr. was born. He weighed five pounds, nine
ounces, and was nineteen inches long.

"You have yourself a healthy baby boy, Mrs.
Buttermark," said the doctors.

"I believe it," I said breathlessly. When they brought
Johnny-Boy to me for the first time, I looked down into
his face and saw the biggest, most beautiful blue eyes
I had ever seen. Then I said to him, "I love you, and
Mommy will take good care of you the rest of her life."

Little did I know, however, how true those words
really would become.

Johnny-Boy

Chapter 2

The Terrible Three Years

John was an excellent child for the first couple of years. One night, when he was just two years old, I put him to bed. He went to bed like a lamb and woke up like a tiger. He was screaming and hollering like a banshee. This began a series of sleep horrors that morphed into no sleep at all.

He always spoke words like *mommy*, *daddy*, *bye-bye*, and *car*. But he was never able to speak in sentences. He walked at eighteen months and was toilet trained at two years old. All motor skills were normal. But I was concerned about his hyperactivity and took him to the pediatrician. He examined John and said there was nothing wrong with him. So I accepted his diagnosis.

The next three years were the worst in my life. John never sat still. Television did not occupy him; neither did toys. He ran to and fro, hollering like he was possessed. So I took him to a gated park/ball field and just let him run around until he seemed to be getting tired. But Johnny only slept three hours a night. He also took a one-hour nap in the early afternoon every day. That meant that I got the same amount of rest as Johnny-Boy. I hated to get up in the morning with him, as I didn't want to have to face another long day.

As a matter of fact, I became so depressed that I thought about ending my life and taking Johnny with me. One morning, about 3:00 a.m., Johnny woke up. My husband and I were both sleeping, but I was the one who got up.

"Are you sure you don't need me to go be with him?" asked John.

"No." I groaned. "You need to support the family and go to work in the morning. I have it taken care of." I really did *not* have it taken care of. I stared at the sheets as my husband fell back asleep. My eyes must have looked hollow. Empty. That's how I felt without sleep and rest.

I trudged to Johnny's room and grabbed his hand. He was already bouncing like he was on a pogo stick. I took us to the car. I drove and I drove, not knowing where I was going. I really wanted to end our lives, and I thought about driving off the bridge. But a voice told me,

No. Stay. Absentmindedly, I drove back home, pushing the suicidal thoughts out of my mind. I thank God for giving me the strength not to do that and to go on.

I used to take Johnny to the zoo during the week when he was a toddler. My favorite spot in the zoo was the aquarium. I would pick Johnny up and sit him on the rail so he could look at all the colorful fish species with me. All of a sudden, two of the most beautiful fish swam by. They were as big as saucers, and they were flat. They were a rusty orange in color, and across their brow they had a Turkish blue line. They reminded me of people with round faces, and they were called diskus. This inspired a trip to the fish store.

"Where do these diskus fishes come from? They have blue lines like this"—I drew a picture on a napkin—"and they look a bit like people."

"They come from a lake in Africa," said the employee. "We can actually get some in the store if you'd like."

"Oh, could you? That would be so wonderful. Just two, so they each have a friend. And what about a tank? I want a beautiful cherry-wood thirty-gallon tank. Is that possible?"

He assured me that it was, and I counted the days to seeing the completed tank. When he called me into the store, the tank's construction was complete, and two diskus were already plopped in.

"Remember, these fish only eat a certain kind of shrimp," the storeowner told me. "I have one bag complimentary for you."

"That's wonderful. Thank you so much!" Both Johnny-Boy and I were excited to feed the fish and put them in the house.

To pass the time in a more relaxing manner, Johnny-Boy and I would watch the fish in the tank. He began to say the word *fish* and point to them. After two years with the fish, I noticed several large eggs, like jumbo caviar, floating in the corner of the tank. I got so excited that I called the owner of the fish store. He came right over to the house and said, "I don't believe it. These fish don't usually mate in tanks like this. This is lucky!"

About a week later, the eggs were getting ready to hatch. While I was sleeping, I heard a splash and a little voice saying, "Fish, fish."

"Oh, Lord. Please no." I jumped up out of bed and ran into the living room. Instantly I saw my son sitting in the tank, trying to catch the fish. The eggs were scattered all around the fish tank, and the two fish were swimming frantically around Johnny. That was the end of my fish. I was so heartbroken.

During Johnny's three years before kindergarten, he would run out of the house, and I would have to chase after him and bring him home. I finally decided to put locks on the doors that kept him in…for a little while. Then around midnight, my doorbell rang. I jumped up and ran to the door with my heart pounding. I paused by the door and noticed the lock open on the floor.

"What the heck…Johnny managed to open the locks on the door by himself?"

I opened the door, and one of my neighbors was standing there with him.

"We were coming home and saw a streak of white. Turns out it was John in his pajamas crossing the boulevard."

"Oh no, you're joking!"

"No, Lucy. We grabbed him and brought him home at once."

I thanked them repeatedly before turning to Johnny-Boy. "What will I do with you?" I had to put the locks up as high as I could so that even if John got on a chair to try and reach them, he wouldn't be able.

At the end of three terrible years, Johnny finally started to sleep all night. Thank you, God! But there was one big catch: his father had to sleep with him. For the next seven years, that's exactly what his father did. At least we all got some much-needed rest, and with rest came more patience and peace.

Chapter 3

Pain and Discoveries

The long-awaited day arrived. Johnny-Boy was headed to kindergarten.

"Be a good boy," I reminded him, straightening his backpack, "and listen to the teacher." Johnny had been flying around like a fighter jet, too ecstatic with the concept of seeing other little children. "Now sit still so I can hand you your lunch." I secured a brown paper bag in his hands.

When he walked out the door and waved back to me, a swell of excitement rose to my throat, but nervous butterflies intermingled with it. I knew Johnny-Boy was special. But I hoped he would fare well.

Wrong. He lasted only one day.

Not only that, but the Board of Education suspended him from going to all schools at the age of five. "We suggest you have him evaluated by a mental health specialist," the note said.

The nervous butterflies invaded my body, and I bit my lip. What other options did I have?

I did what they suggested, and he was evaluated by (who I'll call) Dr. Jones. We settled into his office, which was more reminiscent of a funeral home with its drab, seemingly ancient furniture. We settled on a gray leather sofa and looked at the doctor.

"Hi, Mrs. Buttermark, John." He nodded curtly to Johnny-Boy, already wiggling in his seat.

"So it's my understanding he was suspended." Behind his black-rimmed glasses, he already examined not only John but myself. I shifted uncomfortably. *Tell me something I don't know.*

"The teachers judged him to be too hyperactive and 'unteachable,' as he has no attention span. He's been like this the past three years."

"Leave the office," he said abruptly.

I took one glance at Johnny before I rose from my seat and nervously sat in the hallway. After ten minutes, he called me back in and asked me to take a seat. In the meantime, Johnny-Boy was running around the room touching everything in sight.

Dr. Jones looked at me with his upper lip slightly curled. He put his hands together and gave me that same judgmental gaze over his glasses rims.

"Mother, you and your husband will have no life together if you don't institutionalize him. He belongs in the Willowbrook State School. If you don't do this, your husband will divorce you. Your son John has a slight retardation, is somewhat autistic, and is emotionally disturbed. I think *you* have a lot to do with it."

His words punched me in the stomach, and the sensation rose to my throat. I cleared my throat, between a cough and a moan, and could only stare.

I don't think anyone can imagine how I felt.

I sat in the chair, the silence only broken by Johnny-Boy's babbling. He and I briefly made eye contact. His blue eyes shone with glee. My Johnny.

After what felt like hours, I looked up from my wringing hands and spoke up. "Who are you?" I whispered. He looked puzzled. "Who are you to act like you are God in my son's life? How many parents have you told this to…and they *listened* to you? How can you put your head on a pillow at night and sleep?" My voice shook but rose in intensity.

"Let me tell you, Doctor, I will try my damnedest to bring my son to his full potential until he is eighteen. If that doesn't work, I will seek other means. He is my responsibility, and when he is eighteen, I will bring him back to you so you can apologize. How dare you."

How dare he. How dare he.

The next five years were very trying, but I prevailed. It all began with just Johnny and me.

"Don't worry Johnny-Boy. You're getting your education. I'll just have to teach you myself."

I tied Johnny to a chair at his waist with my husband's belt. This way he couldn't move around, and he would sit and look at the television like that. I did the same when we sat down to eat. I thought, *Maybe I can teach him to respond to me if he's in the chair.* For the next year, I sat Johnny in the chair and belted him in. I would sit across from him at the kitchen table and teach him.

The first thing I did was point to him and say, "Your name is John Buttermark, and you live at _____, and your telephone number is ___," and I would have him repeat it over and over again, pointing at me.

After one year of this, the miracle happened. At the table, he abruptly said, "My name is John Buttermark. I live at ____." His first sentence. From that day on, he spoke more than single, isolated words. He could converse. Even to this day, when Johnny introduces himself to someone, he says the same thing. "Hi! My name is John Buttermark!"

I took John to the park. He was running and running. He just didn't stop. I was nodding off, hoping to use this chance for a quick and restful recovery for myself. A park department employee named Terry was there and was watching Johnny. After a minute of puzzled glances, she walked over to me with her arms crossed.

"Why isn't your son in school, if I may ask?"

I shifted on the bench uncomfortably and glanced up at her with my prematurely aged eyes. This was always an awkward topic, but I told her the truth.

"He's expelled. I can't afford to take him to a special school." I expected her to shrug and walk away, sorry she asked. But her face crinkled into a smile, and she said, "I have a solution for you. Not a school by any means, but I run a camp for kids with Downs Syndrome in the summertime. I would be honored if you brought John."

Of course, I said yes. "I'm thrilled to hear it!" I said, imagining Johnny running around outside with similar peers. Sure enough, he went, and that's when Johnny started to grow mentally and verbally even more than he had been.

One day, I was reading a story in a magazine about a children's neurologist who was coming to Columbia Presbyterian Hospital from California. He only came to see patients once a year, so I immediately called the hospital to try to make an appointment for Johnny.

"Columbia Presbyterian Hospital, this is Shannon," said the young voice on the other line.

"Hi, my name is Lucy Buttermark. I read about the neurologist from California. When is he coming? I was hoping for an appointment for my boy."

"Ma'am, I'm sorry. The doctor is already booked. Nothing is available."

A brick fell into my gut. Before I knew it, I became desperate, and my eyes filled with tears. "Please, I need you to try and fit him in. For any amount of time! I'm desperate. I don't know what's wrong with my boy." I rambled on like a crazy woman.

"Look, I'll tell you what. I'm going to call you back and see if there are any strings I can pull. Give me your name one more time and your number. I'll get back with you."

I told her twice not to forget and hung up. Unable to move from the phone, I sat on a nearby stool, watching Johnny from afar. To my luck, I didn't wait too long.

"Lucy, we were able to squeeze you in." The best news I'd ever heard.

The day I took Johnny to the hospital for his appointment was a wonderful day. The doctor saw my son for forty-five minutes, and then he called my husband and I into his office. He told us, "He will never be a doctor or a lawyer, but he will be a self-sufficient and fine young man if he gets the proper education."

My husband and I hugged in relief. He prescribed medication, and Johnny became calmer than he had ever been his entire life. But he still had to sleep with his father.

Even though he was calmer, he still became frustrated. He bit his hands and would bang his head against the wall when I didn't understand what he wanted. If he had an earache, he couldn't express it to me. I would say to myself, *Why me? All of my friends and my brother's and sister's children are normal. Why me?* But later, I would see why.

Chapter 4

We Need a School

Since the doctor told me that Johnny should have a proper education, I became determined to find a good school for him. So I checked out private schools in the area. The cost of going to one of these schools was over ten thousand dollars a year, which I definitely could not afford. Then I brainstormed. I thought, *I know that I am not the only one in this position who has a child that needs special education and can't afford it.*

So every day I would take Johnny by the hand and ring everybody's doorbell in the well-to-do areas of Staten Island, where there was plenty of money. The scenario would go something like this: I'd gently knock, and usually a housewife answered in all her glory, or a maid would fetch her. Once they were at the door, they stared down at my wiggling child and me. "Hi, my name is Lucy Buttermark," I'd say. Then I'd tell Johnny to show off his sentences. "Hi! My name is John Buttermark." Again, I'd turn to the doorway. "Do you have a child who is hyperactive and autistic?" By this point, many people slammed the door in my face. This happened many times, and I finally gave up. But always in the back of my mind, I wanted to create a school.

When John was seven-and-a-half years old, my second son, Michael, was born. He was also a healthy, normal boy. Things somewhat improved. Michael was docile and slept as much as every mother dreams her child would sleep.

Years passed, and we were a happy four-person family. But in my opinion, Johnny still didn't have the education he deserved, the education I knew Michael would attain with no issue. However, when Johnny was twelve years old and somewhat calmer, I received a call from the Board of Education. They said they were opening a school for the children that were suspended from school. They notified us that there would be a meeting, so my husband and I attended. There we met a few other parents who had children like Johnny, and we all bonded. We laughed and cried at memories of trying to teach and socialize our children—we truly instantly glued to one another. There were six sets of parents altogether, so we made ten new friends.

Then a miracle happened. As we were getting ready to go to bed one night, Johnny had just brushed his teeth. He sat there continuing to look in the mirror as my husband called him to come to bed.

"Tonight you go to sleep with Mommy. I'm a big boy now."

John told me that he sat in disbelief but called me shortly thereafter. "Lucy! You wouldn't believe what Johnny said!"

I ran from Michael's room and, as usual, braced myself.

"What's the fuss?" I said while entering the room, seeing Johnny standing beside the bed.

"Johnny, tell your mom what you just said."

"I'm a big boy now."

"Yes, you are, dear!"

"No, that's not the exciting part," John said. "Johnny said I could 'sleep with Mommy' tonight."

My eyes stretched open, covering half my face. We jumped up and down and told Johnny what a big boy he was. What a relief! My life became more normal than it ever had been. Michael, the new baby, was a good little boy. Johnny was in school every day. He was no longer hyperactive, and he was speaking clearly. Johnny liked school and came home every day and told me what happened in his classroom in his own way. The peace lasted…for a little while, at least.

John was in school for one year when he started coming home with black and blue marks on his back, arms, and legs. I was wary.

"Johnny, how was school today?" I greeted.

John slumped in a seat, lacking his usual enthusiasm.

"Johnny?"

"I don't want to go back to school anymore," was all he said, pouting and peering down at his hands. This was highly bizarre for him; he loved school and always chattered about it excitedly.

I brought him to school and decided to take matters into my own hands. I approached the gray-haired lady in the brown cardigan, ready to squeeze answers out of her.

"I don't know where the bruises came from," was all I could get out of the teacher. She stared me down, wanting me to shoo. I wouldn't give in.

"But when John left for school the previous day, he was fine," I insisted. "No bruises anywhere on his body. He certainly did *not* get those at home."

"Mrs. Buttermark, I do *not* know where your son got those bruises. I know nothing about them."

Accepting that I would receive no answers from her, I was bent on seeking them out myself.

Every day when John came home from school, I waited in the rocking chair by the fireplace, ready to question him. One particular day, he shyly opened up.

"A big boy pushed me on a mat and jumped on me."

"What? Come here, Johnny." I took his arms in my hands to check for bruises. However, I noticed that there were white stains on his clothes. "What's this?" I asked him. John stared at me with his honest blue eyes. He was silent.

But then it hit me.

I sent John to school the next day, and I marched up to the school myself minutes later. I knew what time John had gym class, so I looked in the window to get a picture of what was going on. Immediately, I saw a big boy masturbating on top of my son. He was about fifteen years old and much bigger than Johnny, who was small for his age. I was enraged. The anger inside me boiled, unable to be contained.

As I threw open the door, I saw two teachers standing in the corner talking. They were not paying any attention to what was going on in the gym class, only looking inward on each other. I wanted to slap them then and there, but I first ran to my son.

"Get the hell off my son," I said, grabbing Johnny by the hand as soon as he did. It took every fiber of my being to not do horrible things to that child.

Now it was time to let the teachers have it. I pulled Johnny with me and stood facing the two chatting teachers. I could feel the heat rising to my head.

"You people are obviously neglectful with these children. You're not watching them at all."

Their eyes narrowed, and they opened their mouths to reply. I wouldn't let them get a word in edgewise.

"This is a disgrace. I'm taking Johnny out of this rotten school today. He will *never* come back. Maybe one day you'll actually consider doing whatever the hell you're paid for."

I told Johnny to come with me, and we stormed out of the gym that he would never see again.

That's when I really started thinking seriously that I had to create a school. I got in touch with the parents I had met at the Board of Education meeting and told them the story. They too were upset with the school, but I felt as though I was at square one again. Even though I single-handedly gave the school a reputation for incompetence, I was the only parent to pull my child out.

We checked out other schools and found one that we liked, but it was in another state and had a long waiting list. The school was completely funded by the city, state, and federal government. We requested a meeting with the director of the school to obtain information as to how he started this school. He agreed to help us start a school but told us we would need more than two children. The name of this particular school was Eden. One other parent and I contacted the other four sets of parents. All of the parents got along well together, and we made the decision that it was now or never.

We contacted a lawyer who was a very good friend of ours, and he advised us as to what we needed to do to get started. First we needed to get charted, and then we needed a school or room for the kids. The lawyer found a room for us on the grounds of a seminary on Staten Island. We went to see every politician on Staten Island, begging for monetary assistance to get started. They all agreed to help us but told us that we had to be in existence for two years before we would become eligible for any kind of federal, state, or city funding. We certainly had our work cut out for us.

We hired a director, an assistant director, a speech therapist, and six special education teachers who specialized in dealing with autistic children. We wanted to open a school not only for autistic children but also for children with autistic-like tendencies; my son falls under the latter category. By hiring six special ed teachers, the school would have a one-on-one teacher-to-student ratio.

The arguments I made to our politicians made them see that it would cost less money to service and educate the special needs children and to have them live in their own loving homes. Otherwise they would eventually have to be institutionalized, and that would cost much more money.

We fundraised every weekend by holding dances. The six parents cooked all the food to be served every week at the Saturday evening fundraiser. We held raffles to raise money too. My brother, Gregory Perillo, is a world-renowned artist who donated many of his paintings for the raffles. As much hard work and coordination as these efforts required, we had a blast doing it.

All of our hard work and dedication finally paid off. The State of New York came through for us after two long years, and we received the funding needed to keep our school open and running. We were a success! We named our school Eden II after the original Eden school.

Now that the Eden II school was up and running smoothly thanks to the wonderful teachers and parents that worked so hard and so well with the children, Johnny was flourishing. Barbara Deloretto of Eden II used to come after school and read and write with Johnny. She proved invaluable; she gave me her time to come teach Johnny one on one as well as teach him how to behave. She gave him rewards for good behavior and academic progress. Soon he was no longer hyperactive, and he developed quite a vocabulary. He was able to hold conversations with everyone, and he was very well spoken.

If Johnny had the opportunity to be educated as he is now, he would have been mainstreamed in a regular school, I thought. But I was so grateful that he had come as far as he had and that he still continued to grow. I also realized that if Johnny-Boy wasn't the way he was, we would never have contacted the other five sets of parents, and there would be no Eden II. So many other children would not have been allowed the opportunity to learn and grow as Johnny had. I feel that God gave me Johnny-Boy for that reason: to help other children and to give hope to other parents who had children like him.

I look back on the years and on the wonderful people who became my friends. It is sad to realize that so many of them are now divorced because the stress and strain of raising a special child was too much for their marriages. It was the opposite in my family. Having a special boy brought my husband, my son Michael, and myself closer. The one reason that enabled us to proceed with business as usual was our acceptance of Johnny the way he was and to realize that it was up to us as a family to help him reach his full potential. We all gave him a lot of love, we were consistent, and we supported him in every way possible. We gave him that one big chance.

Now there are three Eden II schools on Staten Island and four groups home that benefit hundreds of clients. There is also one Eden II school on Long Island.

Currently, a new large school is being constructed that will serve all the clients of Eden II under one roof, rather than being scattered here and there. The new school consists of a pre-school, middle school, and adult programs. Eden II was the first school for autistic children in all of the five boroughs. I served as president of Eden II for four years and board member for fifteen. The school that started with only six children has become something that really blossomed. I consider this venture to be one of my greatest achievements.

Chapter 5

Johnnyisms

Growing up, John was notorious for what I call "Johnny-isms." I always thought I could fill a book with our colorful stories and crazy experiences (which is what I ended up doing, of course). In reflection, I can see how hilarious, absurd, and wondrous these situations are, even as scary as they were at the time.

Age three: When Johnny was three years old, I belonged to a bowling league. One night, when I was bowling, my husband was in charge of watching Johnny-Boy. He said he kept walking over and pointing to his throat, and he couldn't figure out why.

Finally, my husband whipped out a flashlight, picked John Boy up, and put him on the table. He shined the flashlight down his mouth, and to his amazement, he saw a straight pin sticking flat in his throat. With that, he picked up our son and ran to the car. He scurried away in such haste that he forgot to put on some pants.

As he proceeded into the emergency room, you can imagine that he received some stares.

"What are you doing out of bed? Here's a gown. Cover yourself up," said an exasperated nurse. She unfolded a hospital gown for him right there and prepared to help him in.

"No, no," my husband said, shaking his head. "I'm not here for myself. I'm here for my son. He has a pin caught in his throat! I need to see a doctor." My husband was so quick and concerned about Johnny that he didn't mind being in his underwear.

Once the doctor looked into Johnny's throat, he tried three times to extract it. The third time was successful.

"Sir, if the straight pin was left, it would have punctured your son's jugular vein, and he'd have bled to death," said the doctor seriously over his spectacles.

Although Johnny-Boy was wide eyed, my husband was glad he didn't know the severity of what befell him at that time.

Age four: When John was four years old, we decided to take a trip by car to Florida to visit my parents. On the way we would stop for gas, and we would all get out of the car to stretch our legs. I would hold on to Johnny's hand, but one time he managed to get away from me and ran across I-95. It was a miracle that he wasn't killed, as God was good and there weren't any cars coming at the time. And there were no cars barreling by as I ran across the street for him. Raising John was very stressful and expensive. It was always an adventure for my husband, Michael, and myself as well, but we all survived.

Age six: I told you that my dad was a tailor and a designer. On Easter, my father had made Johnny-Boy a beautiful navy-blue suit. I dressed Johnny in that new Easter suit, and my father was dressed up in his own matching suit. John stood beside his towering grandfather like a miniature version of him.

"You both look so handsome!" I exclaimed, clapping my hands together. Dad looked proud and nodded while smiling as if to say, "Thank you, thank you. I know it."

"Well, John, you know what we have to do now," said my dad, squatting on his knees and pointing at him.

"Wha?" asked Johnny with his gentle, doe-like blue eyes.

"We need to show off. It's a gorgeous day," he said. He gestured to the kitchen window, where sun-flooded streets and the garden toward the front of our house could be seen. "Let's go feed the ducks."

Johnny smiled hugely in agreement, revealing a couple gaps where his baby teeth had recently fallen out.

I said to my dad, "Are you sure that you want to do this?" because John was only six years old at this time and was very hyper.

My father answered, "Absolutely!"

I shrugged and gave them the bread to feed the ducks, and off they went.

Within an hour, they were back. My father was soaking wet up to his knees, and Johnny-Boy was wet to his chest. I tossed down the newspaper I was reading and stood up from the chair.

"What on earth happened to you both? Let me get some towels." I scurried away to the linen closet while Dad explained.

"John ran into the lake, so of course I had to run in after him. I don't know what made him do that!" My dad shook his head and wrung out his pant leg.

"Well, Dad. I hate to say this, but I *told* you so!"

Age seven: One day, we were heading out of the house for errands. Johnny and I walked along the street until I halted.

"Why did you stop?" Johnny-Boy asked. Rummaging through my purse, I shook my head.

"Mommy forgot something in the house. Stay right here, and don't move," I instructed.

Johnny was shuffling his feet on the front porch when I glanced back at him in the doorway. That was the last I saw of him. When I came back out, Johnny was nowhere in sight.

Oh, God. My stomach dropped, and my tongue dried up. Before I knew it, I was bolting down the street. "Johnny-Boy! Johnny!" I shouted to my left and right, as loudly as I could. If I roused neighbors, so what? I searched the neighborhood and couldn't find him. A cluster of yellow hats materialized in the distance. I ran closer and saw they were construction workers.

"Have you seen a little boy run through here? He's seven and special."

"No, ma'am, I haven't," said one of them.

Then I went to all the neighbors asking the same thing. Again, nobody had seen him.

"Johnny-Boy! Hello? Where *are* you?" I screamed his name, but there was no answer.

I was beside myself. I called my husband to come home from work. When he came home, we searched the neighborhood again and still couldn't find him. We finally decided to call the police. We explained to them that Johnny was mentally challenged and was missing. The police and all the neighbors formed a search party. It was getting dark out, and I was horrified that no one had seen him and that he couldn't be found. Around ten o'clock that night, a man came running up the block toward the police officers and my family.

"I don't know if this is pertinent to your situation or not, but I'm hearing strange sounds from a manhole down the road," he said breathlessly.

"What are we waiting for? Let's go!" My husband urged us on, and we ran over in an instant.

John, the man, and the police officer squatted down and managed to lift the cover off the manhole. And there was Johnny-Boy all wet and dirty and crying. To this day, we don't know how he got there.

That same year, he went into my next-door neighbor's house. Rose's husband, Joe, wore a toupee, and he belonged to a band. You guessed it—Johnny went into their bedroom, saw the toupee, and took it. Nobody knew that he did that…until I heard Johnny in the bathroom in our own house saying, "Pretty hair."

"Johnny is probably admiring himself," I said with a laugh. I walked into the backyard, and I heard Joe yelling out the window to Rose.

"Did you see my toupee? I'm late, and the band is waiting for me!"

With that, a light bulb went off over my head. I ran to the bathroom, opened the door, and there was Johnny looking at himself in the mirror with the toupee on his head.

I expected a surprised look, but he smiled at me warmly. "Pretty hair, Mom."

Without a word, I grabbed it from Johnny's head and ran outside to give it back to Joe.

I wrung my hands and felt terrible. "Joe, I am so sorry. You let this boy out of your sight and he ends up in strange places."

Joe wasn't mad at all. He said, "That's okay, no harm done," and smiled at me.

Age eight: Because my husband was a plumber and excavator, he owned a backhoe machine. When my husband came home from work, he would park it in the driveway behind my car.

We had just purchased a new car the day before this particular incident. My husband had just come home from work, parked the backhoe in the usual place, and came in the house to eat the dinner I was preparing. But suddenly, a growling and grinding sound was heard.

"Do you hear that noise?" I asked, looking up from the pot of boiling water and giving John a confused expression. John pushed himself back from the table and crossed his arms.

"That sounds *just* like a backhoe. Someone in the neighborhood must be having a sewer put in...and to think they even didn't call me to do the job! They know I live so close by!"

My husband then marched to the windowsill and, aggravated, pushed the lacy curtains aside. Suddenly his jaw dropped and eyes widened.

"If it isn't…Johnny!" My husband yelled Johnny-Boy's name in shock and raced outside, and I scampered behind him with my stained apron still on. And lo and behold, there was Johnny-Boy on the backhoe, lifting the boom from one side of the new car to the other side. My husband froze in his steps. When he collected himself, he got on the backhoe and shut it off.

Oh well, that's Johnny!

Johnny was fixated on the television program *One Day at a Time*. He particularly liked the character Julie. She had a ponytail that fascinated him. So he would take a piece of rope, string, or sometimes my hairpiece and would pin it on his head and make believe that he was Julie. He shook back and forth so the "ponytail" would swing like hers. I would have to hide my hairpiece from him.

"Johnny, this is mommy's. She needs this. It is not a toy." In the end, I had to throw it in the garbage because he played with it constantly.

My hairpiece wasn't the only discarded mass of hair. My husband bought Johnny a gorilla costume, and when he wore it, he thought he was actually Chewbacca. We had to throw that in the garbage too, as he wanted to wear it day and night.

"I thought he would only wear it at Halloween!" my husband said as we tossed it in the garbage can. "Leave it to Johnny!"

Combine this love of suits with superheroes. If there's one thing Johnny loves, it's Batman. He has two authentic rubber Batman suits. He is only allowed to wear them for very special occasions—one being Halloween. When he was younger and had no fear, he would climb out of his bedroom window and make believe he was Batman with his suit on. All the neighbors would ring my bell and tell me that Johnny was on the roof. I would have to call him in, and thank God he listened. He certainly always kept us on our toes.

Age ten: Johnny was around ten years old and was going to Confraternity of Christian Doctrine classes (CCD) every week. After communion lessons, he received his communion and confirmation. The bishop preached the whole mass and chose Johnny-Boy to hold his staff out of the church. Tell me if that was not God's doing?

One day when Johnny came home from CCD, he started asking me questions about the devil.

"Mom, if God lives in heaven, where does the devil live?"

I put my book down and looked at him seriously. "Johnny, the devil lives down there"—I pointed my finger to the ground—"in a place called hell. The devil is very bad, and he wants to take the good people away from God because the devil doesn't love God."

"That's not nice," said Johnny. His eyes widened at the idea of such evil.

A week or so passed by, and I went shopping. When I came home, Johnny and his dad were in the backyard. I noticed that Johnny was digging in one corner of the yard.

My eyes narrowed, and I walked over to him.

"Johnny, what are you doing? This is such a deep hole." I stood at the edge and looked down at him shoveling in it. It was already about three feet deep.

"I'm getting to the devil, Mom. I'm gonna tell him that I love God. It isn't nice that the devil doesn't love God." He turned back to his project, furrowed his brow, and continued.

Can you believe it? Johnny wanted to make everyone love God, including the devil. And he wanted everyone to love one another. That's why my Johnny is an angel without wings. I truly believe it. Sometimes I say to myself that everyone should take a lesson from Johnny-Boy. He doesn't lie or curse. He is always respectful and always has the biggest smile on his face. And when he tells you that he loves you, it comes from the bottom of his heart. Whenever I ask Johnny to do something for me or my husband—like putting out the garbage, vacuuming, and making his father and brother espresso—no matter what he's doing at the time you ask, he stops what he's doing without a thought and does as he is asked. He never says "in a minute" or "later." He is just such a good human being. That's one of the reasons why I call him an angel without wings.

I will never forget the day when Johnny was about ten years old and my younger son, Michael, was two. My next-door neighbor was having a christening party in the back yard. The only barrier that separated us was a fence between the two yards. Next to the fence I had a picnic table. All of the food and all of the party guests were in the next yard; chatter, laughter, and music floated to our ears.

All of a sudden, I started hearing people screaming and yelling.

"Move! Move!"

"Ahh! The food!"

I was sitting on the patio in my yard and looked over in their direction because people started running away and slamming the door of the house. There was Johnny-Boy standing on top of our picnic table with the hose in his hands. He was directing the spray at the people in the next yard. They were all soaked, and the food was ruined. That was one of the many things Johnny took upon himself to do.

Teenage years: John was fifteen years old at this time and loved rope fish, so we bought him one and put it in a big tank in his room. Johnny was so happy and would spend the day watching it swim. By this time, Johnny was speaking very well as he had a one to one at Eden II and had really progressed. On the day before Thanksgiving, I decided to get ahead and knock out a few dishes. I scurried around the kitchen in a gravy-soaked, flour-dusted apron as any mother on the holidays. Johnny had been upstairs with his fish, Charlie, but suddenly barreled downstairs.

"Mom! Mom! Charlie is swimming funny. I think he is sick."

"Johnny-Boy, I have to cook some of the food so we can eat sooner tomorrow. When your dad comes home, he will take you to the fish store and fetch medicine for Charlie."

"Okay," he said, slumping over and traipsing upstairs.

I returned to the kitchen and measured out a half cup of flour. Johnny came downstairs again. His face was white as a sheet.

"Mom, I think Charlie is really, really sick."

I repeated what I told him before. He turned around and went back up to his room.

That boy… I shook my head. *What does a sick fish even look like?*

Once more, I immersed myself in the kitchen, still cooking, and I heard the distant wail of sirens. I looked out my dining room window and saw an ambulance coming up the street toward my house.

"What a shame that someone is sick just before Thanksgiving!" I said to myself, shaking my head. Fishy enough, the sirens grew louder and louder but didn't fade away into the distance. All of a sudden, a set of paramedics stormed up my driveway. Alarmed and shocked, my body tensed up.

"What in the world? They have the wrong house!" I exclaimed as I walked to the door.

Three burly men busted in, pushed me to the side, and asked, "Where is Charlie?"

Johnny-Boy came running down the stairs.

"Up here! Charlie is upstairs having a heart attack!"

Without question, the paramedics ran up the stairs. I stood there with my mouth open in complete disbelief.

I was mortified. I knew it would be just a moment before they found out and demanded answers from me. Sure enough, the paramedics walked downstairs with stern faces.

One accosted me and said, "Miss, don't ever let your son call us again for a sick fish."

No sooner had he said that than the police appeared to our left. The EMTs explained to them what had happened.

"Ha! No way. That's hilarious!" The cop bellowed with laughter and then turned to Johnny. "Son, here's the thing with 911. Only dial if it's an actual *human being* that needs emergency help."

The cops laughed again, but I was still appalled. After it was all over, though, I realized just how funny it was.

I remember the time when Johnny had finally learned how to ride a two-wheel bicycle. He repeated, "I can ride a bike! I can ride a bike!" He must have excitedly chanted it hundreds of times.

One day he was riding it around the block, and two boys approached him. They pushed him off the bike and beat him up. Two of the neighbors saw what was happening. They chased the two boys away and brought

Johnny home. Johnny told me what had happened, and he was very upset. It was then that he asked the dreaded question: "Mommy, why did God put my brain in backward?"

My stomach went numb, and I inhaled sharply. "Johnny, God did not put your brain in backward. You are so special, Johnny-Boy, and that's why God made you special. He loves you so much!"

He broke my heart that day.

Not only was Johnny's awareness of his condition heartbreaking, but also it's difficult for a sibling to grow up in a home with a mentally challenged brother. I had to give most of my attention to John Boy. I wasn't there for Michael most of the time, and it still breaks my heart.

I used to say to Michael when he was little, "Your brother is in the front of the house. Go outside and watch him." The neighborhood kids frequently mocked John because he was different. You know how kids are.

He did as I asked and stayed outside with him. Once when they came back into the house, I noticed that Michael had a bloody lip and his eye was swollen.

"Michael, what happened?" I rushed over to his aid and gently caressed his lip.

"The other kids on the block were making fun of Johnny and were hitting him. So I had to fight 'em."

Even though Michael was seven years old and Johnny was fourteen, he would defend and protect his brother.

I remember one Fourth of July the kids on the block had firecrackers. They put them in a bunch on the street and put a pail over them. Michael heard the kids say that they were going to let Johnny-Boy sit on the can and light the firecrackers. With that, Michael took his brother by the hand and took him home. Michael always protected his brother, who was seven years his senior, but still very much like a younger sibling in various ways.

Recently I spoke to Michael, who is now the father of three beautiful girls. I told him how sorry I was that I was not there for him when John was growing up. He answered me by saying, "Mom, you did the best you could. Let me tell you that without my brother Johnny, I would not know how to laugh when things aren't going well, I would not know how to love unconditionally, and I would not know how to have compassion. So John gave me an education that money could not buy."

Chapter 6

The Accident

Generally, all was well by the time John was sixteen—for a while, anyway. He had joined a new program called On Your Mark. At On Your Mark, Johnny played basketball and went swimming twice a week after school with children like him. He made many great friends and became very social, much to my relief. Johnny went to his program on Friday nights just for the purpose of socialization! Then he went on Saturdays for athletics. Johnny was always busy, and he loved it.

He had blossomed into a fine young man. It was now time to bring him back to the psychiatrist from Mental Health. I called for an appointment and said it was for me. The day of the appointment, I took Johnny-Boy with me. It was my day of redemption. When we marched into the office, I approached the receptionist. I tapped on the glass.

"Hey there. I'm here for *my* appointment."

She shuffled papers and opened a folder. "Mrs. Buttermark?"

"That's right."

"Go ahead and have a seat. The doctor will see you in a few minutes."

John looked from me to her. "Mom, why are we here?"

"For mom to see the doctor." This was a new concept for him, but he accepted it.

In a few minutes, the nurse called me into the office. Before I rose from my seat for my noble purpose, I leaned over to Johnny.

"Stay right here until I tell you to come into the office. It'll just be a couple minutes." I winked at him.

Smirking, I went in to the doctor's office and sat down in front of his desk. He was looking down at some papers as I sat opposite him. His judgmental gaze only hardened with the stringent wrinkles that carved around his mouth over time. He looked up at me and said, "Mrs. Buttermark, how can I help you?"

I replied, "Twelve years ago, I visited you when my son was five years old. You examined him, and after your examination, you told me, 'Mother, you and your husband will have no marriage, or you will get a divorce if you don't institutionalize him. You cannot keep him home.'"

With that he asked, "Did you take my advice?"

"I'm not finished talking to you," I snapped. "When you told me to put my son in an institution, I asked, 'Who are you to play God? This is his life. How dare you! How could you put your head on a pillow and go to sleep at night? And how many parents have you told that to and listened and institutionalized their children?' Well, Doctor, I did not take your advice, and I have something to show you."

With that, I got up and called my son into the office. I introduced him to John.

John looked at him, extended his hand, and said, "Nice meeting you, Dr. Jones. My name is John Buttermark," just like I taught him.

"Sit down, son," he said. Then he began interrogating him.

"Where do you go to school?"

"Eden II."

"How old are you? Where do you live? What do you do at Eden II?"

John replied confidently. "My parents and five sets of other parents founded the school for us."

The doctor was very impressed; his eyes widened in a way I had never previously seen. He actually looked awake. He asked John to wait for me in the waiting room. After shutting the door, the doctor sat across from me and apologized to me.

"I didn't realize that John had that potential. Your husband and you have done a great job."

"Doctor, with faith, love, and patience, anything can be accomplished. John is a perfect example." With that, I got my satisfaction.

I couldn't have been happier for Johnny, until he was eighteen years old. One day at school, Johnny was walking with his class and teachers around the seminary grounds. I was told one of the brothers from the seminary had just come off a new tractor lawn mower. He came over to the children and shut the mower off, but he forgot to shut down the blades.

"Johnny, would ya like to go for a ride on my new tractor lawn mower?" he asked.

"I can't because I have a math test after our walk," he said.

"Aw, no fun. Teacher, can't Johnny go for a ride?"

Sure enough, she waved Johnny to go along.

"All right, go ahead and hop on up. Climb over the blades." The brother got on the tractor, not realizing that he forgot to shut them off. What ensued was a spattering of blood that would never be forgotten.

The blades ripped into Johnny's pants and chewed the back of his right leg from just below his knee all the way down to his ankle. Johnny and everyone screamed, and the brother quickly shut off the blade. Johnny was bleeding profusely, and the teacher called for an ambulance. He was rushed to the nearest hospital.

Meanwhile, I was at home; my husband, John, had just come home for lunch, and the phone rang. It was the director of the school. I was surprised but pleasant.

"Oh, hi there. What seems to be the problem?"

His voice was hushed but frantic. "Miss Buttermark, get over here immediately. Johnny had a terrible accident. His leg got caught in Brother's lawn mower."

I could feel the blood drain out of me. My vision dissipated into streaks of light, and I had to sit down. All I could picture was the tractor lawn mower I had seen on the grounds of the seminary, and I pictured Johnny falling off it. I pictured him with his arms stretched out to protect himself and prevent himself from falling. I could picture his legs and arms being caught in the blade.

I gave a shuddery exhale and grabbed my chest. "Director, does he…does Johnny still have his arms and legs?"

"Just come to the Doctor's Hospital ER as quickly as you can. I'll meet you there."

I hung up and instantly shrieked my husband's name. "John! John!" I stumbled to the backyard, still clutching my heart. I know he knew just by looking at my face that something terrible had happened.

When I told him, he started to cry like a baby, and so did I. We just hung on to each other for support. The rest of the experience was an excruciating blur. We composed ourselves and robotically got in the car. I called one of my neighbors to take care of Michael when he came home from school.

On the way to the hospital, a bird hit the windshield of our car, and I thought that was a sign of bad luck. I felt as though everything was going in slow motion. All I wanted was to see my son. I was beside myself with worry.

When we finally got there, we ran to the emergency room, and I heard someone say, "Cover the leg so the parents don't see it."

I finally saw my beloved son. I couldn't tell his lips from the rest of his face, as he was so white. When he saw us standing there, he started to cry. Words of comfort eluded us. My husband cautiously walked over to John and lifted the sheet covering his leg. Over the handkerchief covering my face, I saw my husband make a gurgling sound and pass out right there.

"Is this guy having a heart attack?" I heard someone yell.

All the while Johnny screamed, "My leg is on fire! My leg is on fire!"

"Doctor, can you *please* give him something for his pain?" I was desperate. I knew if my husband was fainting, this was quite an injury.

The doctor shook his head gravely. "Johnny needs immediate surgery, so I can't give him any pain meds right now."

I was beside myself as we had to wait for a plastic surgeon to come to the hospital, and he would be delayed because he was currently operating on someone else.

Meanwhile, my Johnny was wailing in terrible pain. Luckily they stopped the bleeding, and I was able to look at his leg. It looked like he had been attacked by a shark. His leg was so mangled, but I was so grateful that it was just his leg. Imagine that.

I stayed with Johnny for over two hours until the plastic surgeon finally arrived. During that time I sang to him, prayed with him, held him, and hugged him to try and keep his mind off the pain he was feeling. Finally, after waiting for four hours, the plastic surgeon arrived. He examined Johnny's leg, and I held my breath in anticipation.

"Mrs. Buttermark, there's quite a lot of dog feces in the wound. This presents a danger of going blind from fecal infection. I'll put him on antibiotics in hopes of defending against that.

"The other danger is that there's glass in the wound, so I'll have to extract both good and bad tissue from the leg. John has lost tendons and ligaments, so there's very little muscle left. We need to be aware of the possibility of John never walking again, or if he does, dragging his leg."

At this point, I was numb. I just wanted my son safe and sound.

Johnny was taken into surgery, which lasted six hours. The plastic surgeon did his best to piece his leg together and hoped there was enough good tissue left to close the wound in his leg. During the surgery, Johnny's heart stopped, and they had to use the electric paddles to bring him back. He had lost so much blood that he had to have blood transfusions. I wondered when this torture would end.

When Johnny came out of surgery and woke up from the anesthesia, he looked at me and smiled. He said, "I feel good now. Everything is going to be all right." He inspired me even in the darkest moments.

Chapter 7

Recuperating Trooper

For the next ten days, my sister and I took turns staying with Johnny during the night. John was in the hospital for one month, and he was our trooper. The nurses and the doctors loved him. Johnny made them smile with his special ways, always pleasant when circumstances weren't ideal. The day John was released from the hospital, everyone who could get out of their room stood in their doorways to wish him well and to say good-bye. As he was wheeled down the hallway, everyone clapped. Johnny even stopped to shake some of their hands. It was as if he was a hero or someone important. Johnny loved every minute of it. Like I always say, "To know Johnny is like the sunshine of your day." He makes you feel so good with that big smile on his face and the care in his heart.

The very next day we had to wheel John to the doctor's office. The doctor was so kind that he let Johnny go in the back way into the office so that he would not have to wait long. He helped John onto the table and sat down. The doctor proceeded to take the bandage off his leg. He finally got down to the end of the bandage when John's flesh came off. Sickly green gangrene had set in the wound. My heart went to my throat.

The doctor told us that Johnny had to go back in the hospital for further treatment. A wild look settled in Johnny's eyes.

"No, Mom, I don't want to go to the hospital. Please, can you take care of my leg?"

I looked at the doctor and said, "Doctor, is this a possibility?

"Lucy, are you willing to do everything I tell you to do to take care of his leg? You'll still have to bring him to me every day so I can check on it."

"Please, Mom! Please, Mom!" Johnny cried repeatedly.

I took a deep breath. "Yes. I will do it."

You have to realize that this was my son. The leg was open, and I had to take care of it no matter what. No mother wants to see her child suffer, let alone take care of such a ghastly wound. But I committed myself to do it, and I did.

The next year was quite difficult. Every morning I would have to unwrap his leg and help him get out of bed. He would put one arm around my shoulder and hop to the bathroom. The water and medicine were already in the tub. He would sit on the toilet seat and put his right leg in the medicated water. I would turn the Jacuzzi on and pull a stool next to him. Then I would tell him stories.

"Johnny, did you ever hear about the brave boy who got hurt on a motorcycle?"

"Nuh-uh." He looked at me attentively, turning his head as far from his leg as possible.

"Well, this boy's leg was badly bruised and cut just like yours. The boy was very brave, and he let his mother take care of him. Every day the boy's leg would close and get better and better. The boy's leg got better quicker because the boy was so brave. After a while, the boy's leg improved so much that the boy was able to walk."

Johnny-Boy liked that story because he knew I was talking about him. We would pray together and sing together for thirty minutes while his leg was in the Jacuzzi. After supper we would have to clean and soak the leg again. Before each changing of the leg, I would be downstairs on my knees asking the Blessed Mother to give me some of her strength to change the dressing on his leg. After all, the Blessed Mother had strength to see her Son die on the cross. Believe you me; she *did* give me that strength. Not that it was easy. After changing the dressing, my body trembled like the ground during an earthquake. It was powerful and unstoppable. I could only go downstairs and cry, wishing I'd forget the vulnerability of his leg. I saw everything in that leg. I saw the bone. I saw the meat in it.

As promised, I brought Johnny to the doctor every day so he could check on his leg and see if I was doing a good job.

One day, the doctor said, "Lucy, I have this new medicine. I will give you a sample and a prescription for it. You must put this medicine on the dead tissue." He gestured to the gray dead tissue on Johnny's leg.

"This medicine will destroy the dead tissue. Please, Lucy, don't put the medicine on the good new tissue, as it will destroy it."

Oh, God, I thought. *Help me to do this.* Such a procedure seemed beyond my anxiety-ridden, clumsy self.

But I did it. Every day was so difficult. One day John and I were in the bathroom singing. I noticed that he kept glancing at his leg. I stopped singing and asked him why was he staring at his leg.

"Mom, doesn't it look like a shark bit my leg wide open?" Every now and again, this upset him.

But I said, "It really does. Sharks are cool! Remember that old shark book?" And I would lead him into a new topic.

After soaking his leg for thirty minutes, I would help John hobble back to the bedroom, and there I would have to put the medicine in his leg while Johnny-Boy lay on his stomach.

Every day he would tell me, "Mom, you are doing a great job. You can press hard. You won't hurt me."

He had such patience and courage himself that it made the cleaning better for me. He never complained.

"I will walk soon. You'll see, Mom." His hopeful words nestled by my heart, a bundle of hope in our rough times.

I brought Johnny to the doctor's office every day for two months so that the doctor could check how his leg was coming along. The gangrene was gone, and the leg was healing. The doctor was very pleased. After the first two months, I continued to take Johnny to the doctor twice a week. Then finally, I took him once every two weeks and then once a month. An end was in sight.

Michael and his friends would come to visit John.

"Mom is doing a good job with my leg, guys!" I heard him say. This never failed to glue a smile to my face for those eleven months. I don't know how I would have had the patience and the will to withstand the pain that my son did.

During the course of Johnny's recovery, my father and mother came up from Florida to see him for a week. My father was sitting with me having lunch, and I couldn't look up at him or hardly eat.

"I know Johnny's special and can't live like Michael. But now he's disadvantaged physically. I wish I knew why God did this." I kept spooning and pouring my soup rhythmically, resting my hand on my cheek.

My father pushed aside his bowl and lifted my chin. "Lucy, I just want to leave you with this thought—it might not sound hopeful. But you will see this come to be. Out of *every* tragedy, something good will come of it."

"I don't think so. Poor John and his one leg."

But my father was a very wise man. I wanted to believe his words as fervently as I did as a child.

One day when Johnny was soaking his leg in the Jacuzzi, he asked me for a glass of orange juice.

"This means I have to go downstairs, Johnny. Are you going to be all right while I'm gone?"

"Yeah, Mom! Yeah."

I trusted he'd be safe and swiftly went downstairs. As I grabbed the orange juice from the fridge, I heard Johnny-Boy muttering to himself.

"Worms…my leg."

Pausing, I tilted my head in the direction of the staircase.

"Worms are coming out of my leg!"

I ran upstairs and looked at his torn leg in the bathtub. "Johnny, what's going on?" Before he could respond, I saw for myself. Hundreds of long, thin, blue tendrils were squiggling out of his leg. And they really did look like worms. I ran downstairs and called the doctor. He told me that what was coming out of his leg were his veins. He also said, "Do not pull them out or cut them, just stick them back in his leg with a Q-tip."

I could actually feel the color draining from my face with those words. *God help me*, I prayed. But I did as he told me, and then I calmed Johnny down by making a joke of it.

I said, "Your veins *do* look like worms," and he laughed.

As with life, the only reason we pulled through the whole mess was because of each other and our faith.

Chapter 8

Walking to Recovery

The next few months were difficult and boring even though Johnny had a lot of company. His friends from school and my family came often to visit. I thank God that John's eyesight wasn't impaired, but I still worried about whether or not he would always drag his foot. Johnny-Boy, on the other hand, wasn't going to wait to find out.

"Mom! I want to go outside today." His leg was still opened, but not all the way. "I wanna try to walk around. Can't you take me to the playground?"

"We're not doing anything until I call the doctor first," I said. Walking to the phone, I made my daily call.

"Lucy," he knew my name and around when I'd call by this time, "what's going on today?"

"I'm just wondering something. Is it all right for John to walk? He's sitting here waiting for your answer about going to the playground."

"John knows his own body, and if he feels like he can walk, he will. He'll let you know. It's worth a shot."

So I put Johnny in the wheelchair and wheeled him to the playground down the street. We arrived, and he sat watching all the children play. His brow furrowed, and his jaw set.

"Well, Johnny, what are we going to do?"

He squeezed the armrests on his chair. "Help me up. I wanna walk."

"Oh!"

I was surprised that when push came to shove, he wanted to. I slung my arm around his back and grabbed his arm with my other hand. He took one step with his left foot, and as he took a step with his right foot, I noticed that he dragged his ankle/foot.

"What's…no." He couldn't even comment on the dragging because it upset him too much. I grabbed him under the shoulder and sat him back in the wheelchair. An anchor dragged my heart down to the pit of my stomach.

"Mom! Let's go to the park. I wanna walk this time."

Two weeks had passed. I wanted Johnny to have another chance, so I pushed him in his wheelchair to the playground, and I sat on the bench for a while. The entire time I bit my lip and prayed. *God, if Johnny can't ever walk again without dragging his leg, please help him to accept it.*

"Let's go, Mom. I want to walk." He got up from the wheelchair beside the bench and started to walk, but he still dragged his leg. He turned toward the wheelchair with his lower lip protruding and sat back down.

"Johnny, do you want to go home and try again later?"

"No." It wasn't open for discussion. So I sat down on the bench watching all the other kids laugh and play while John sat the wheelchair. I noticed Johnny staring at a boy about ten years old. He was walking along a white line on the concrete. He was walking the line as if he was on a tightrope, putting one foot directly in front of the other.

Johnny turned and said to me, "Mom, you see that boy walking the white line with one foot in front of the other? I want to try that, and maybe I won't drag my leg anymore."

I was willing to try anything at that point. I wheeled Johnny over to the white line, and he stood up. I pushed the wheelchair away, and Johnny stood on the white line. He put his right foot in front of his left foot, his left foot in front of his right foot, and held both his arms outstretched to balance him. He pretended that he was on a balance beam, but he was on the ground, walking the white line. The best thing of all was that he was not dragging his foot. You could see from the smile on his face how happy he was. It was a smile I hadn't seen in a long time; it beamed a ray of hope on anyone who witnessed it.

He walked that line for one hour that day. The sweat was pouring off his brow.

"John, it's time to stop. Enough is enough. You need to rest!" I brought him home and called the doctor to explain John's progress. The doctor thought Johnny was amazing to have figured out how to walk without dragging his foot.

After that, we went to the playground every day so Johnny could practice walking the line. Eventually the walk that Johnny invented became his own walk, and Johnny's natural way of walking no longer existed. Johnny-Boy was on his way to bigger and better things. It took him one month of practicing his new walk every day to be able to walk without dragging his leg. Sweat poured in torrents off his brow, but he never gave up. The doctor was amazed when he saw Johnny walking into his office for the first time without a wheelchair and without dragging his foot. He was so impressed that he asked my permission to take Johnny to a meeting that night. It was with the doctor's class of interns. He wanted to show them what an accomplishment Johnny had achieved. Naturally, the interns couldn't believe Johnny's progress; they were absolutely amazed.

I sat in the corner, unable to purse my lips and contain the grin bursting on my face. Recalling the whole ordeal of the year, I remembered questioning God: "Why did Johnny have this horrible accident? Isn't it bad enough that he was born different?" I knew that God had a reason for everything, but why my Johnny? Then I thought about what my father had said to me: "*Out of something tragic, something good will come.*"

And this is only the beginning, I thought as I saw doctors shake his hand.

Chapter 9

Exceeding All Expectations

As the days went by, Johnny became more and more confident. He was no longer dragging his leg, and his new way of walking was working for him. One day Johnny told me that his leg hurt when he didn't move it. So I found someone from Eden II that ran in the races on Staten Island to work with him. Her name is Joann Gerenser. She is now the director of Eden II and whom the board and I had hired as a special speech therapist for Eden II. Joann would take Johnny running three times a week after school. He became stronger and stronger.

The Staten Island Advance Five Mile Run was coming up, so I asked Johnny if he would like to try it. Of course he said yes, as he was always willing to try anything. When Joann wasn't available to run with him, I would take him to the track at the College of Staten

Island. I would run, Johnny would run, and Michael would run. I was a much slower runner than my two sons, but I was with them, and that's all that mattered.

When Johnny's leg finally closed, it healed with only scar tissue over the bone. The right leg was much thinner than the left, especially near the calf of his leg. The doctor told my husband and myself that Johnny's leg would need reconstructive surgery. He said that he would take flesh from his thigh and put it on his calf right down to his ankle because the scar tissue would eventually open. He also said it didn't have to be done right then but down the road. We tucked that away in our thoughts for the future and looked forward to the race.

Soon the day of the race approached us. Johnny completed the whole race, and he enjoyed every minute of it. His running time was one hour and fifteen minutes for those five miles. Considering his handicap, I think he did a great job, and I was very proud of him. Johnny was proud of himself too and asked when the next race was coming up. He ran the next race, called the Pepper Martin Race, and did well. Johnny found that running made his leg stronger, and he felt much better. He ran those two races every year for the next eight years.

Once eight years passed, he was tired of running and was interested in doing something else. I suggested to him that he try the Special Olympics, as there were so many different venues that he could try. Johnny decided to join the swim team. He was picked to go to the state games to compete in the swimming. Johnny was always a great swimmer and won the gold medal for swimming that year. My husband, Michael, and I could not believe the courage that Johnny-Boy had to go on. He competed in the Special Olympics for swimming for the next two years and won a gold medal each time. We were all so proud of him.

Johnny felt his possibilities were endless. He was restless to try new things but excelled at each one. The next thing Johnny wanted to try was gymnastics. He brought home the gold medal in that too. Then he decided that he wanted to try weight lifting. He broke all records in his division in the state games. He has received so many gold medals in weight lifting that the judges announced him as "Batman the Weight Lifter" and still continue to do so.

This was only the beginning of Johnny's success. He showed that one could overcome anything with determination. No matter what handicap you have, nothing should hinder you from living life to the fullest.

Chapter 10

Batman the Weight Lifter

Johnny achieved his lifelong dream. He was Batman. Just as Batman had strength and abilities as a superhero, Johnny discovered his nugget of strength within him: courage, determination, and a can-do attitude. Plus, he was strong physically, as you can imagine.

Johnny always loved Batman and has been obsessed with him right up to the present day. He has a shrine in his room to his beloved Batman. He has every Bat Mobile that was ever made, every doll, and every other character from the Batman series. He has all his posters of Batman, and all his books are Batman books. There is also a bat hanging from the ceiling. His bedroom is decorated with a Batman bedspread and draperies. He has every Batman DVD in existence. He calls his room his Bat Cave. If something didn't go right for him at his Dayhab program, like if someone became upset, Johnny would come right home, go into his room, and tell Batman all about it. When he came out of the room, he would be feeling much better.

"And here's Batman!" roared the judges when Johnny came out for contests. Johnny threw his fists in the air Rocky style and grinned from ear to ear.

"I am Batman!" he said. He was living his dream.

Every year in June on Father's Day weekend, he would go upstate to the weight-lifting competition. They would bench press on Friday and dead lift on Saturday. That was when John was at his best. As I mentioned, he was a force to be reckoned with: he benched 235 pounds and dead lifted 375 pounds. His weight at the time was 178 to 180 pounds. He easily got the gold medal for bench press and dead lifting. He also got the gold medal for all around in his division. My husband, John, was also a weight-lifting coach, along with Dennis Tobin. They would go upstate with the other young men on the weight-lifting team, and quite a few of our boys brought home the gold, silver, or bronze medals.

When Johnny-Boy started weight lifting, my husband and I became friendly with Richard Salinardi, who was the area coordinator of Special Olympics, and with Jo Ann Certo, trainer for Special Olympics. My husband, John, was very impressed with the team and how they worked out. He decided that he wanted to be involved, so he became certified as a coach and has been coaching the team ever since. Many years later, Michael volunteered to work with the weight lifters, and he enjoyed it so much that he too became a certified coach and is now working with his dad. I cannot describe the rewards we all got from working with the weight lifters. The weight lifters became Johnny's friends, and he grew up with them. The kids who participate in weight lifting and their names and titles are as follows: Anthony Aragona (The Animal), John Buttermark Jr. (Batman), Pat Cogliano (Spiderman), Michael Diel (The Real Deal), Michael Deveney (The Rock), Mark Fairweather (Big Dog), Anthony Fairweather (Big Show), Danny Lane (Dangerous Man), Tim Braisted (The Tornado), and Kenny Tobin (Big Sexy). When the boys are at a weight-lifting competition, they are called up to compete by their weight-lifting name.

Every summer, we invite the coaches of the weight-lifting team, the weight lifters, and their parents to our home for a barbeque and pool party. All together there are about fifty people. We give out our own trophies to the weight lifters. At the party, we have a diving contest and give out a trophy for the best diver. Also, some of them perform. Johnny-Boy puts on his official Batman suit and acts and talks like Batman, swirling his cape and strutting around the yard for all to enjoy. His best friend, Pat, dresses like Spiderman, and they perform their act about catching the bad guys. Also Anthony (The Animal) sings, and Kenny dances. Then the rest of the weight lifters gather around and do their own thing. And every year they say that the party was the best one ever. To watch all the young men happy, laughing, hugging, and sharing love together is a joy to behold. As a bystander, you can actually feel the love shared between them and the joy they feel being together like this.

"When's the next party?" they all ask in chorus.

"Next year, guys. It'll always happen once a year."

"Aw, I can't wait!" Johnny says.

"Yeah! I hope the year goes by fast. These are the best," say the others.

I want to tell you that in spite of all his involvement in sports, it was hard for Johnny to have a good friend, like a *best* friend. He grew up with his weight-lifting friends, of which there are six. But he never had a *best* friend until Johnny outgrew Eden II after being there fifteen years. I decided to send him to Darren Nangano's *DayHab* for a change of scenery. This is a program that

On Your Mark runs. And this is where Johnny met his best friend, Pat.

They are inseparable. They go to each other's houses, the movies, and their programs together too. Pat loves Spiderman and John loves Batman. They call and talk to each other on the phone. One of their favorite things to do is hang out in the pool in the summertime. Pat's mom, Camille, and I have become very close friends also.

"I'm so happy they found each other," Camille always says.

"Me too. They're perfect together."

One summer day, it was so sweltering that I told Johnny, "It feels more like an oven out here. Let's get out of this stuffy ol' house."

"Pat has to come too," said Johnny. I wouldn't have it any other way.

Johnny and Pat were sitting by the pool, and I was nearby reading. They were relaxing in the shallow end of the pool and had their heads together so close you'd think they were discussing the meaning of life.

"Pat, when I get my driver's license, I'm going to get a black car, and it will be just like Batman's car."

Pat nodded and stared attentively as he always does. Johnny is boss.

"It's going to be my Bat Mobile. And that's what I'll call it, my Bat Mobile. I'll use it to pick you up from DayHab!"

With that, Pat said, "When I get my car it will be orange, just like General Lee's in the *Dukes of Hazard*, and I will pick you up one week, and you can pick me up the next week. We will take turns."

I snorted into my book and pulled my gardening hat over my head. *They are little boys in men's bodies. They are so innocent, so loving, and caring. You just can't help loving them.*

Jack-of-All-Trades, Master of All

We discovered that there was a program in ice-skating for the Special Olympics. The program was being held at the SI War Memorial Skating Rink on Staten Island. It was a training program for figure skating in the Special Olympics.

I opened the flier on our kitchen table and looked up at Johnny, who had just come back from running.

"Hey, Mom!" he greeted cheerfully, settling himself in the red corduroy recliner.

I was excited to tell him. I knew he was a born athlete.

"Johnny, there's an ice-skating training program. You're so good at everything you try, so would ya wanna give this a shot too?"

His eyes lit up and danced playfully. *Of course* he was interested! Johnny never says no to anything.

Motherly instincts kicked in, and I had to ask to be certain: "Do you think you can manage with your bad leg, though?"

"Psh, yes, Mom. It hasn't ever stopped me and won't stop me."

So off we went on a Sunday morning to the rink. We rented special skates for figure skating and held our breath after Johnny put them on and headed out to the ice. He was a natural at figure skating and didn't fall *once* all the time he was on the ice. The instructor was impressed. The whole time she couldn't sit still, rubbing her hands together and grinning when he finished.

"All right, Lucy, I have a proposition for you. I want to personally train Johnny for the Special Olympics figure skating competition."

Naturally I was thrilled. But I looked at Johnny for a sign of interest, and he said, "Yes, Mom!"

Every Sunday, we went to the rink for Johnny's lesson so he could practice for two hours. In addition, he weight lifted three times each week. Johnny did that for ten years. He got so good at weight lifting and so good at figure skating that every year in February, we would go to Buffalo to see him compete in figure skating. And every year he competed in weight lifting he brought home the gold in both sports.

Johnny-Boy and his dad and I went to Buffalo to compete. Johnny did a perfect performance there. He didn't forget a single move in his program. His spiral was the length of the rink. He won the gold medal that day (February 1996). When the ice skating competition was over, Johnny went on to weight lifting.

We got a call from Special Olympics that Johnny was chosen for the Nationals in South Bend, Indiana. We were all so excited. We flew to South Bend, Indiana, three days before the competition so that Johnny could practice at the rink he was competing at. I noticed that he was favoring his leg.

"Johnny, does your leg hurt?"

He continued gliding by. "My leg is cramping up, but I'll be okay, Mom."

In Johnny's eyes, the glass is always half full.

The day of the competition came, and Johnny placed fourth. Johnny did not get a medal that day, but he took it like a true sportsman. In fact, it made him stronger and more positive. Skating was over for the summer, and Johnny was weight lifting again. He got gold medals in all three of his competitions. Come September, Johnny started practicing for figure skating once again. To say the least, he had a busy lifestyle. There was figure skating on Sunday mornings, weight lifting three times a week, and Eden II every day.

Soon June came around. I walked past the rosebushes outside to our mailbox and saw Johnny received a letter from Special Olympics. I couldn't wait for him to come home from his program to open it, tapping my fingers on the table and frequently peeking out the window, hoping he'd walk out. But soon he bounced through the door, shouting, "Hey, Mom!" We opened the letter together and both squealed. It read as follows:

Dear John:

On behalf of New York Special Olympics, I would like to congratulate you on being selected to represent Team USA at the 1997 World Games in Toronto, Canada. You have received the honor from the hard work you have dedicated to your sport and your gold medal performance at the 1996 New York Special Olympics Winter Games in figure skating.

You and your family should be very proud of your accomplishment. You have been selected from among the finest athletes throughout New York State. We wish you the best over the next several months as you begin your preparations for the road to Toronto.

Mary Calamari, Director of Programs in the New York City Office, will be your contact person. She will be forwarding all information to you as it comes from Special Olympics International. You can reach her at 212-661-3961. She will be happy to answer any questions you may have.

The entire family of the New York Special Olympics supports you. Congratulations and go for the Gold.

Sincerely,
Barry A. Bornstein
President/CEO, New York Special Olympics

When I read that letter to Johnny-Boy, his face lit up. I hugged him and told him, "Mommy is so proud of you, and I love you so much."

He looked at me with the biggest smile. "I know you are proud of me, and you are the one that worked so hard to help my leg heal and made it all possible for me to do this. I love you, Mom, and thank you for all your hard work. All the sadness you went through, it's all behind us now."

And again I say that my father was so right when he said, "Out of something tragic, something good comes."

When my husband and my son Michael came home from work, we gave them the letter to read. They hugged Johnny and started jumping up and down. Watching my family unify under the joy of Johnny's progress was a sight to behold. I felt so blessed that day—and every day I spent with Johnny.

Chapter 12

All Publicity Is Good Publicity

As I sat reading by the window, watching the golds and reds of the leaves float and dance down to the faded grass, I thought about how good life was. Two years before, Michael had gotten married, and Johnny was his best man. He was thrilled to have this honor, and I was thrilled have a daughter-in-law who is truly like a daughter to me named Peggy. A year later, Michael's first daughter was born, and they named her Briana Lucia. When Briana was baptized, Johnny was her godfather. Two years after that, Caitlin was born, and three years later, Lauren was born. Peggy, Michael, and the girls live directly behind us. We share one big back yard with a large swimming pool. In the summer, the girls have their friends over to swim and hang out. They love to play with their uncle Johnny. They tell their friends, "Wait till you meet my uncle Johnny!" Every one of them loves him, and my granddaughters are so proud of him. John is like a little boy in a man's body, so they all get along so well.

Johnny had exactly one year to prepare. I hired a coach to teach him all of the elements he had to perform. The coach's name is Debby; she was a professional figure skater and was thrilled to prepare Johnny for the competition. In the beginning of his training, Johnny went three times a week at six o'clock in the morning to Bayonne, New Jersey. We would get up at four thirty, drive to Bayonne, where Johnny would practice for two hours, and get off the ice at 8:00 a.m. I would drive him home, and he would change and get ready to go to his DayHab program. He would get home from DayHab at four in the afternoon, and we would have dinner. No matter how tired he was, he insisted on going to weight-lifting practice every Tuesday and Thursday. Then on Sunday morning, he would have ice-skating practice for another two hours. Friday nights he went to On Your Mark for his socialization program. He was a very busy young man, and he never let his bad leg get in the way of what he had to do. He had a passion deep inside him that no one or nothing could take away from him.

The red and gold leaves fell, winter's ice melted, overfilled flower buds burst into colorful bloom, and at last, the summer sun sat high in the sky. As the summer went by, Johnny's skating got better and better. Channel 4 contacted us, and we had the pleasure of working with Mary Carillo. She had won a gold medal in swimming and was now a news commentator for the Wide World of Sports. September finally arrived, and Channel 9 News contacted us. They heard about Johnny going to the World Games in Toronto for the Special Olympics and wanted to meet with us at the skating rink in Bayonne, New Jersey. Monica Pellegrino was the newscaster to interview Johnny. I contacted Richard Salinardi, the area director of Staten Island Special Olympics, and I invited him to come with us for the interview. Johnny's coach and Mr. Salinardi spoke about how dedicated to skating Johnny was, and in spite of his terrible accident that destroyed his leg, he overcame it all and worked hard to get where he is today. My husband and I were also interviewed. After Johnny's practice was finished, the people from Channel 9 News came back to our home to interview Johnny.

"John, how is it possible for you to skate with such a bad leg?" they asked him.

This was his answer: "Because God helped my mom to make my leg better so I could do this."

They looked at him with awe. "You are such a good young man, and we wish you the best of luck."

"I'm going to bring home the gold medal! You just watch."

Then after that, Channel 5 and Channel 11 newscasters interviewed him, and he was on their news programs as well. Everyone that interviewed Johnny could not believe how he performed so well with such a bad leg. Johnny just kept on smiling.

Now that he was on television, he became a super star to his friends and family. He was very proud of himself, and so were we. Now that things were so great, they only got greater.

In the meantime, our local paper, *The Staten Island Advance*, came to interview Johnny and take pictures. They gave him a big spread, including his story and pictures of him ice skating at the rink. Under the photo, there was a comment about Johnny skating with all his heart. That was so true because everything Johnny did, he did with all his heart.

The article read:

With All His Heart in Red Letters

You get lost after a while in the laughter, and you forget what you are even doing here. They are telling you one story after another, and soon you start forgetting the questions you wanted to ask. You put your notebook aside. You came here to interview John Buttermark Jr., a thirty-three-year-old man who has been selected to compete in the Special Olympics World Wide Games this coming February. He will be competing as a Figure Skater in the games, which begin February 2 in Toronto. After fourteen years in Special Olympics, Buttermark has made it all the way to the top to Team USA.

You sit in the living room of this two-story Graniteville home talking with John Jr. and his parents, Lucy and John Sr. The parents start telling you about the adventures they have experienced with their "Johnny-Boy," as they call him. You listen and just lose yourself in the joy of their laughter. Johnny Buttermark Jr. is mentally challenged (mentally he is thirteen years old, so his mother says). His parents have been aware of his disability since he was two years old. It has not always been easy raising this boy. Some of the stories are not at all funny, like the times he would run out of the house then dash across the highway. Or the times he was so hyperactive that he could not be left alone.

But ever since he started attending a specialized school twenty years ago, and since he became involved in programs like the Special Olympics and On Your Mark, Johnny has been blossoming. He is a much calmer individual than he was as a child. He is the life of any conversation. He is also quite an athlete, having excelled at running, weight lifting, and figure skating to the theme of *Rocky* as his music of choice. Johnny skated his way to a gold medal at the New York State Winter Games in Buffalo this past February. He is one of 130 athletes competing in the '97 World Winter Games.

"It's exciting to see the progress," said Debbie Koellner of Sunnyside, a skating instructor who coaches Johnny. "He knows how big Toronto is. He knows how much it means."

This is Johnny's story of triumph. A story that has his parents so proud that they have rented a catering hall for a good luck party. It's the story that has him dancing in the living room to explain his skating routine. It's the story of his practicing his figure eights and his arabesque spiraling three times a week at the War Memorial Rink in Sunnyside. Every great success story has to include a triumph over adversity. In

Johnny's case, you would think that his developmental disability would be enough of an obstacle.

But there is more. There is another disability, one that's a little tougher to talk about and a lot tougher to look at. It involves lawn mower, a razor strap, and Johnny's right leg. It happened in June of 1979, and Johnny can remember the incident vividly. He remembers the pain. "I lost a lot of blood. I couldn't believe I did that." His parents remember their son's screaming, they recall his going into shock at Doctor's Hospital, and they remember when his heart stopped beating during surgery. Doctors revived Johnny, although his leg was still in terrible shape. It took a full year for his leg to close up. Mrs. Buttermark says even today, there is no muscle from the middle of his calf down to his ankle. There are no tendons back there and no ligaments. Just bone covered by skin. Johnny was told he would never walk again. But less than two years after the accident, he was running in the SI Advance Memorial Day Run. Seventeen years later he is lacing up his skates for World Class competition. He is defying logic in what he is doing.

"Do you ever talk to your leg to tell it what to do, Johnny?" [news person] asks.

"I talk to my leg and tell it not to hurt and it obeys my command." He goes on: "My grandfather always said to me and my mom, 'Out of something tragic, something good comes,' and look what we have here—we have the World Games."

John Buttermark, Sr. tells a lot of stories, but he also gets quite serious when he talks about his son. "You've got to love this guy," he says, "and I'm not ashamed to take him anywhere." On January 10, his father will be taking his son to the Staaten in West Brighton, where 200 of Johnny's closest friends and relatives will gather to wish him good luck in the Winter Games. Technically it's a good luck party. Really, though, it's just a chance for a lot of people to tell one man how much they love him and of course to tell a few stories. They'll probably talk about the time that John Sr. took his son Johnny to the beach and he disappeared, only to show up about two hours later wearing a birthday hat. He had wandered into someone's back yard not realizing there was a search party out looking for him. Or they'll tell about when Johnny was running in a Special Olympics race, and he was winning, when suddenly he looked up and noticed a parachutist floating to the ground. Johnny slowed down and watched the parachutist as the other runners ran right past him. They'll talk about the gold medal that Johnny gave to his ailing uncle, and about the medals he has given away to people he defeated in competition. Or they will talk about the time he tried to revive his dog with mouth-to-mouth resuscitation after the dog had a heart attack (the dog, Lucky, was not revived). There will be so much to talk about that day, so much laughter. This is Johnny Buttermark's life, to have such a life. "I tell you he makes us happy," John Sr. says. "He's a good boy. He tries with all his heart. A lot of mothers and fathers would give up, but I would never give up on this kid."

There were two large pictures of John in that article, and underneath the picture of John doing the spiral, it read, "John Buttermark Jr. has overcome more than his share of obstacles to compete in the Special Olympics World Winter Games Figure Skating Competition in February. Family and friends know him as a person who always tries." Under the other picture of John holding his arms out on the ice, it read: "John Buttermark Jr. brings joy to family and friends whether he is working on his skating moves for competition [top photo], or just being himself."

Chapter 13

The Unforgettable Party

After flipping through photos from Michael's recent wedding, a light bulb flickered over my head.

Johnny is never going to get married, so I want to do something special. Why not throw him a huge party before he goes to the Special Olympics?

I stowed the thought away in the back of my mind as we continued to interact with the media, but soon my husband was in on it, and it was mutual: *we must do this*. This was Johnny-Boy's big hoorah, and he certainly deserved it. Michael, Peggy, my husband, and I were so excited about doing this for him. We booked the Staaten for the night of January 10, 1997, only a little over a month away from the World Games. The day finally came, and there were two hundred guests there to celebrate Johnny. We had a buffet table that served everything from soup to nuts and then some. There was a turkey roast, roast beef, mussels, clams, shrimps, pasta, vegetables, salad, stuffed mushrooms, artichokes, fried zucchini, soda, and all kinds of mixed alcoholic drinks (not for the special needs children—that is a big no-no). The media came too, and the event was televised on local TV.

After all the guests were seated, it was time for Johnny to make his grand entrance. The DJ rolled the drums and announced, "Here's Johnny!" The doors opened and in he walked, dressed in a tuxedo, wearing an Uncle Sam's hat of red, white, and blue and swinging around a red, white, and blue cane. As he walked around the room, the DJ played the theme from *Rocky* and the smoke machines went off. As he walked around the room, he swung his cane with one hand and waved to all the guests with the other. Everyone cheered as he walked by the guest tables. As you could gather, the theme of the party was based on the World Games and the USA. All the decorations were in red, white, and blue, including the tablecloths and napkins.

When Johnny completed circling the room and the music stopped playing, the DJ stepped up to Johnny with a microphone.

"John, is there anything you want to say to your guests tonight?

"Yes," he said energetically, gripping his cane tighter. *Oh God, what is he going to say?*

He grabbed the microphone and said, "I want to thank everyone for coming to my party. Now let's get ready to *rumble!*"

Everybody cheered; I wiped my forehead. The music played, and everybody got up and danced, ate, and had a blast. Johnny's coach got up and talked about Johnny's hard work and dedication. Michael also got up and said, "I'm so proud of Johnny and always have been. Bring home the gold, brother!" The party was a night neither Johnny nor I will ever forget.

Chapter 14

The World Games

The next afternoon it was on TV. They showed a montage of the party and wished Johnny the best of luck at the World Games. Because of all the publicity, Wide World of Sports called, and they wanted to cover the story about how Johnny overcame his tragedy and to come to Canada to the World Games to cover Johnny's story and his performance. What an exciting time this was for us! I called Richard Salinardi, Joann Certo, and Beth Fromkin, who also volunteered for the Special Olympics. Joann and Beth booked flights to Canada. They were so proud of Johnny, and they wanted to be there to support and cheer him on at the World Games.

The day finally came when Johnny had to leave us. He had to go one week before us with his coach to the World Games. Then it was our turn to leave for Canada.

It was my husband and I; Michael and his wife, Peggy; my two granddaughters, little Briana and baby Caitlin; and my brother's wife, Mary Perillo. The whole family wouldn't dream of missing a thing.

The next day was the first part of the competition. We all got up early and headed over to the arena to cheer Johnny on. We had the best seats in the house. The competitors had to perform specific elements that were required in the first half of the competition. They were judged on each element they performed. The first element was skating forward, the second was skating backward, and the third element was crossovers (that is, crossing one foot in front of the other as you skate around the rink). Johnny-Boy was particularly strong at that one. Then you had to stop short, which was another element. The last element was a figure eight.

We waited in anticipation. I was sure to remember a quick prayer. *Dear God, help Johnny do his best today. He's worked so hard. Thanks for not only helping him heal but for helping him thrive too. We're so proud of Johnny-Boy.* The truth was, I couldn't see Johnny doing anything but his absolute best. Everything he does is with all his heart.

Suddenly, we heard a rumble of static and an announcer clearing his throat.

"Now we have John Buttermark, representing the USA!"

Our hearts were in our throats, but we still cheered loud enough for John to hear. He skated out, gliding gracefully and confidently. We saw a sparkly black blur streak past us; he did the first element perfectly (skating forward). Then he did the second element (skating backward), which was Johnny's weakest element.

"He looks so handsome standing there in his black sequined shirt and skating pants." I couldn't help but brag. He was indistinguishable from a professional.

Johnny looked down, bit his lip, and furrowed his brow. Each part of him, down to the beads of sweat on his temple, was immersed in his performance. He started skating backward skillfully. All of a sudden, he hesitated and then continued on. My heart sank, and I knew it was going to cost him points. But all of the rest of the elements he performed perfectly. Neither myself, family, or friends could have asked for anything better as he did his best in part one of the competition.

Running down to the rink, we had huge smiles plastered on our faces.

"Congratulations, John! That was great!"

"We're so proud. You had an excellent performance."

We rained praises, hugs, and kisses on our boy. Johnny's face looked like it would cut in half because his smile was so huge.

"Thanks, everybody," he said. "But I gotta go back to the hotel with the rest of Team USA."

We wished him well and said we'd see him the next day. "I'm going to win tomorrow," he assured us.

Meanwhile, we decided to wait and see what position the judges would post for Johnny. After plenty of nail biting and praying, the scores came out. First was Mexico, second, Germany, third, Austria. Johnny was in fifth position after part one of the competition.

"Fifth?" I fretted. "But it's almost impossible to move up to third place if you start there." In spite of my initial disappointment, it didn't matter to us. Johnny had already come so far, and we were so proud of what he had accomplished. We went back to the hotel and went out to dinner. We discussed Johnny's performance and prayed that his free style was going to be perfect the next day.

The next morning, we sat at the rink right as the peachy glow of a cold sunrise crept over the land. We saw Team USA arrive and headed toward them. There was Johnny with his big smile looking at us.

We all wished him good luck, and he said, "Mom and Dad, don't worry. I know my program by heart, and I will do it perfect." With that, he kissed all of us and went with his team.

The time finally came, and Canada did well, Russia did well, Austria *didn't* do so well, and then it was Johnny's turn. The lights went down, and the spotlight was on Johnny as they announced him. He came skating in with the biggest smile on his face and stood in the middle of the skating rink. Everyone clapped; then the audience hushed into silence. Music from *Rocky* boomed throughout the stadium, and Johnny began skating. Every move he made was perfect. He did his spiral across the rink, everyone cheered, and he was done. He did it so perfectly, seemingly effortlessly, like he said he would. We all breathed sighs of relief.

"I tell you, he never lets us down," said my husband, and I couldn't agree more.

As the competition ended and we waited for final results, we were bundles of nervous energy, energy that could've melted the ice. My husband and I gripped each other's hands. *He was fifth place yesterday…but nothing less than perfection today*, I thought. *The results could be anything*. And we hoped they were in Johnny's favor. We held our breaths until the long-awaited results came in.

At last, Johnny walked over, sat in the booth with his coach…and we saw he was in third position!

"He got the bronze medal!" I shouted. Michael whooped, my husband's fists shot in the air, and Peggy and Mary clapped their hands. We all hugged one another repeatedly. All of the skaters went to the center of the rink and were given a bouquet of flowers, and then they received their medals. Johnny-Boy looked up at us and threw us kisses from the podium. I can't even begin to tell you what a thrill it was for me to watch my son Johnny standing on that podium. I started crying. My husband, Peggy, and Mike were ecstatic. We all were.

That day was one of the proudest days of our lives, one that we will never forget. The events that followed were one exciting blur. Johnny-Boy came home with the bronze medal. Wide World of Sports interviewed my husband and I and Michael. They put it on international television. They covered the whole competition from start to finish. Johnny was a star, a bright shining star. Everyone congratulated him when he came home with a bronze medal.

The Borough President of Staten Island, Guy Molinari, hosted a reception at Borough Hall, and they asked Johnny to say a few words. The Borough President gave Johnny-Boy the key to Staten Island and proclaimed that day to be John Buttermark day. It was in the papers, and the headlines said:

> In praise of a special man, Borough President honors John Buttermark for his figure skating achievement. It was a great day to be John Buttermark. He'd be

the first to tell you that. "I'm a celebrity," he said smiling. "I feel good about that." John Buttermark, a thirty-three-year-old Graniteville resident and figure skater, was honored in Borough Hall yesterday for his bronze medal finish in the Special Olympics World Winter Games last month in Toronto. Borough President Guy V. Molinari recognized Buttermark's achievements in a ceremony before more than thirty family and friends.

"John is just another one of those great, great stories that makes us understand what life is all about, what life can be all about," Molinari said. Buttermark, whose skating routine was done to the theme from *Rocky*, bounced back from a slow start in the compulsories of the Winter Games. He turned in the highest score in the free style competition on February 6 to earn himself the bronze medal that hung around his neck.

"I'm really good at it and I'm honored," Buttermark said.

Buttermark has also become something of a media darling. After he was profiled in the Staten Island Advance this past December, Buttermark was featured on ABCTV Wide World of Sports and on three local news programs. He has enjoyed the publicity quite a bit. "He says he's a star," said Buttermark's mother, Lucy. "But he's also a lot more, and that's why room 122 of Borough Hall was jam packed yesterday afternoon." There was Richard Salinardi, Staten Island Coordinator for the Special Olympics and Barry Bornstein, President and Chief Executive Officer of New York Special Oympics.

"John is the perfect example of a Special Olympian," Salinardi said. "His sheer joy of competing captivates everyone who watches him. He competes for the sheer love of the sport," added Bornstein. When the community at large honors someone like Johnny, you have achieved what Special Olympics is all about. John has the respect not only of his own peers, but he has the respect of the entire community.

Gregory Perillo, the renowned artist and Tottenville resident, was at yesterday's ceremony as well. Perillo is Lucy Buttermark's brother. "I'm proud of you John Buttermark," said Perillo. "You are an angel without wings."

The Borough President declared yesterday as John Buttermark Jr. Day on Staten Island. The honoree was smiling, joking with Molinari, and making sure that everybody was happy. It was his kind of day. "There is so much more to John Buttermark Jr. than his athletic skills," Molinari said. "There's his big heart and his love for fellow man."

Johnny's celebrity life didn't end there. The very next day, we got a call from the head of the Boy Scouts of America on Staten Island. He had heard about Johnny and all of his accomplishments. The Boy Scouts wanted to honor Johnny by giving him an honorary luncheon. All of the Scout leaders of all the troops on Staten Island were there as well as the president of Special Olympics, Richard Salinardi, as well as the area coordinator, Joann Certo and Beth Frumkin. There were about 150 people in attendance, including my husband, Michael, Peggy, and myself.

After the luncheon, they started talking about Johnny-Boy. They spoke about the courage that he has had, his undying faith, and what a terrific human being he is. Then they announced Johnny, introduced him to everyone, and presented him with an award for the Best Athlete of the Year on Staten Island. Everyone stood and applauded for Johnny. In addition, they presented him with a beautiful medal and plaque.

"Johnny, do you have anything to say to all your fans here?" said the speaker, offering the microphone.

John nodded energetically, took the microphone in his hand, and started to speak. He said, "It is an honor to receive this plaque and medal from the Boy Scouts of America, and I want to thank you for it, and I love all of you." He said it the way he felt it, with all the love in his heart.

After John won the bronze medal at the Special Olympics World Games, he was asked to throw the first ball at Shea Stadium. He not only threw the first ball, but his picture was on the big screen, and underneath it was his name. And it said that Johnny was a Special Olympian. It was all in lights. The image is still lit up in my mind today. Special Olympian, yes. But he was my angel without wings first and foremost.

Chapter 15

Change for the Better

Even though Johnny achieved high honors for his ice-skating performance, weight lifting never left his life. As mentioned, he always went to a weight-lifting competition on Fathers' Day weekend. After this competition, Johnny went on a trip to Hershey Park in Pennsylvania for the weekend. It was August of 1999. He went with his peers and staff. They were walking through the park, and a lady was pushing her daughter in a wheelchair, and she did not see Johnny-Boy walking in front of her. She accidentally hit Johnny on the back of his right leg, which is the leg that he injured so badly. Since Johnny only had bone and skin on that part of his leg, it opened up easily, and blood flowed swiftly. The staff put antibiotic cream on it and bandaged it for him. In spite of all their efforts, Johnny got a very bad infection.

I was lying at home, anticipating Johnny's return. When he walked in, I saw not just him but two other people on his side. They were staff members from the Hershey Park trip.

"Oh, what are you guys doing here? Is everything all right?" I lifted myself from the floral sofa.

"Lucy," began one staff member, "John's had an injury. A woman pushing her daughter in a wheelchair accidentally hit Johnny's leg, and we all know how delicate it is."

"Let me see it." I immediately swooped to Johnny's bloodstained, bandaged leg. I unwrapped and lifted a couple layers of bandage and saw that his wound was red and oozing. "Thanks for all your efforts on his leg. I'm just going to go ahead and call a medical professional at this point." There was no time to waste. The staff said bye to Johnny, and I whisked the phone off the hook.

The plastic surgeon sounded concerned over the phone, and we agreed it was best that he see Johnny's leg "in person" the very next day.

Sure enough, when the surgeon straightened his spectacles and saw the wound, he nodded.

"Is it okay?" I understood the nodding to be a good sign.

"No, it's infected, just as you suspected," he said. "That oozing confirmed it. Debrieving should be the next step."

"What's that?"

"Debrieving a wound means to shave off layers of the scar tissue so that it can bleed. The blood flow will help it heal, along with the medication. His leg currently does not have good circulation because of this scar tissue."

Johnny sent me one nervous glance where he bit his lip, but after that, it was time for him to be brave again.

"You're an Olympian, Johnny," I reassured him. "You're strong and brave. You'll get through anything."

Every week the doctor would debrieve his leg, and Johnny Boy was brave again. This process went on for eight weeks. One day, though, the doctor's forehead crinkled as he stooped to examine John's leg.

"Lucy, this leg isn't healing. The next step is leg reconstruction surgery." He stood up, straightened his frock, and looked us in the eyes.

"What does that involve?" I'm sure I was white as if I was the one who lost blood.

"Basically," the doctor explained, "I'll take flesh from the side of John's ankle and thigh. Then I'll put the flesh toward the back of the leg, where the scar tissue is. And let's hope it takes."

I glanced at poor Johnny and sighed. "Here we go again."

The day came for Johnny to have his surgery. He quietly went in without complaints. The operation lasted four hours, and he stayed in the hospital for two weeks. The doctor said that his leg was doing very well. He had to stay off his leg the whole time he was in the hospital. The only time he was allowed out of bed was when he had to use the bathroom. The leg finally healed, and John started walking again after two months. After four months, he was able to go back to his DayHab Program. Through all of this, John was as patient as ever, and his attitude was as happy as ever. *That's why I call him my hero and my angel without wings*, I thought proudly.

After this ordeal, Johnny did not skate anymore, and that was okay with John. He told me, "Mom, my skating days are over, but my weight lifting days aren't."

"We can always learn something from you, Johnny-Boy," I said. "Your skating era is something to be proud of, and we all are.

Since John had been with On Your Mark for ten years, I thought it was time for him to make a change. I heard that Richard Salinardi opened a DayHab called

Lifestyles, and Richard was the executive director, and it was an excellent program. His wife, Sue Salinardi, is the head of the Respite Program and does a great job too. I called Richard and told him I was interested in sending Johnny Boy to Lifestyles. I made arrangements with him to see the program with Johnny Boy.

"The only way I'll go is if Pat comes too," said Johnny resolutely, hands on hips. I'm glad he was open to it because at On Your Mark, Johnny is the "mayor." That's what they call him because he talks to *everybody*. This is how Johnny complements Pat. Johnny brings out the best in the meeker Pat and looks after him. Every time John goes away with his DayHab peers, he says, "Don't forget my friend Pat. He has to be my roommate," and so John has Pat as his roommate, no questions asked. So I knew I would have to get Pat's mother, Camille, on board. She was and continues to be like family to us, along with Pat of course, so I didn't expect any issue.

I called his mom and told her about the program and that I thought that Pat would do very well there. She took a tour of Lifestyles and so did Johnny Boy and myself. We were all so impressed with the program. In fact, Camille was so impressed that she made an appointment with her husband, Rio, so she could see it again and show him in the process. All of the clients were treated like adults. The staff was so caring and so professional. It includes Nancy Jones, Pat McGee, Joe Joyce, and Anne Daurio. These wonderful staff members are the best of the best.

Johnny liked the greenhouse, so that is where he's now working. Pat liked the café, so that is where *he* works. We are very happy that we made the decision to send Johnny and Pat to this fantastic program. Johnny gets paid for the work he does every two weeks. He is so proud that he is able to earn some money; he finds value in what he does.

No matter what changes Johnny experiences in life, he is positive about each and every one, embracing all his available opportunities.

Chapter 16

Law-Abiding Citizen

One day, John asked my husband and I to take him to a hockey game at Madison Square Garden. "The New York Rangers and the Philadelphia team are playing," raved Johnny. "We gotta go, guys!"

When we got to the game, Johnny Boy was chattering excitedly and pointing to each player. The game started; it was very rowdy, so Johnny fit right in as he cheered for the New York Rangers to win. All of a sudden, in the middle of the game, the players started to fist fight.

Johnny Boy became very upset when he saw it and asked, "Why are they fighting like that? They could get hurt!" He scowled at them and continued to tap my arm and point. "I have to tell the referee to stop them."

With that, Johnny rose up and proceeded down the stairs toward the rink.

"What is our son doing?" asked my husband. I craned my neck as Johnny stormed away.

"We can only wonder," I said, sinking in the bleachers.

When he was halfway down the stairs near the rink, the attendant stopped Johnny.

"Sir, where do you think *you* are going?" He crossed his beefy arms and stood in front of him.

This didn't deter Johnny-Boy. "I have to stop the hockey players from fighting. They're going to get hurt." Johnny looked at the attendant helplessly upset.

He quickly realized that Johnny was special at this point, so his demeanor softened. "I'll tell you what, son. I'm going to go over and tell the teams to stop fighting. Now why don't you go back to your seat and enjoy the game?"

This soothed Johnny, and he did as he was told. That's my son; he is all heart.

About fifteen years ago, we were vacationing at the beach in Florida. We strolled along the boardwalk, gazing at the shops and inhaling the warm and breezy beach air. Johnny was so captivated he kept forgetting to use the restroom, but when we saw some, he knew what he had to do.

"Mom, we gotta go!" He tugged at my swimsuit cover up and beckoned me to them.

"All right, I'm going to go too. Wait for me outside if you're done first."

We went our separate ways, parting at the water fountain that stood in between the men's and women's restrooms. I was finished first, so I waited for John. Just then, a man walked up to the water fountain, lifted up his leg, and stuck his foot under the water to clean all the sand off it.

I muttered to myself, "I sure hope this man finishes washing his feet before Johnny Boy comes out." As you'd expect, right then, out he comes. He looked at the man, outraged.

"What are you doing? People drink from that fountain, and you are washing your dirty feet in the fountain that people *drink* from!"

The man's upper lip curled in a grimace. "Kid, why don't you shut up?"

I muffled a gasp. *I'm about to give this sorry guy a piece of my mind*, I thought. But Johnny held his own. He stomped away, and he saw a policeman on patrol on the boardwalk. He must've told him about the man washing his feet in the water fountain because the officer and Johnny came walking back urgently. All that happened was that the officer wrote the man a ticket and handed it to him.

Ha! Serves him right. I decided to walk over and introduce myself as Johnny's mother.

"Ma'am, everyone should be just like your Johnny here," he said, offering his hand out to Johnny, which he accepted and shook heartily.

"Well, Johnny, it looks like you've done your good deed for today," I said with my chest puffed out like a proud lioness. Johnny was pleased, and we went on our merry way.

Christmas time rolled around, and we were out shopping for our family members. We stopped at a CVS store as my husband wanted to buy cigars.

"While Dad does that, I wanna look at the toys," asserted Johnny. I said okay.

As I stood watching John peruse the selection of cigars, I dreamily eavesdropped on the various conversations around us. The CVS was so packed at this time of day, not to mention this time of year. Suddenly, I heard someone talking heatedly to another woman.

"This lady is breakin' the law! You have to stop her. That's illegal!" I realized that this indignant voice was familiar. "It's illegal to steal toys in your coat!"

I thought I could have crawled in a hole, but it was time for action. With that, I walked to the back of the store, and sure enough, there was a lady standing in the aisle holding her coat closed. Her arms were crossed against her torso so tightly that a pin couldn't have slipped through.

"Johnny, what's going—" Before I could finish my inquiry, the security guards came running down the aisle where we all were.

"Ma'am, I'm going to have to ask you to open your coat," one said sternly.

"Absolutely not. I've done nothing wrong. This guy is evidently special and doesn't know what he's talking about."

"Excuse me, lady," I began, narrowing my eyebrows. In the meantime, Johnny Boy kept insisting that she had toys under her coat.

"If you just get her to uncross her arms, you'll see! She has all these toys in her coat. Promise!"

The lady turned redder and redder, and I thought she'd explode. Finally, she opened her coat. All the toys fell on the floor. Johnny-Boy smirked and yelled out, "I told you so!"

The lady clenched her hands together in two fists and looked like a bulldog. I thought she'd growl right there. Instead, she thrust her claw of a finger at me and said, "Your boy belongs in an institution!"

I put my hands on my hips and laughed. "Lady, you're the one who will be going to an institution." The security guard then took her away to wait for the police.

Later on, as my husband, Johnny, and I were walking toward our front porch with handfuls of bags, Johnny-Boy turned to me. "Mom, I have a question."

"Ask away, dear."

"What's an institution?"

"Johnny, it's a place that you *definitely* don't belong." He was satisfied with that answer.

Chapter 17

More Johnnyisms

The Bed

One morning Johnny came down for breakfast and was unusually quiet. My husband asked, "Johnny, did you wake up on the wrong side of the bed or something?"

With that, Johnny went upstairs and came back down about five minutes later. He told his father, "Dad, I feel so much better. I got up on the right side of the bed." That's Johnny. He takes things literally.

John and His Grandma

On Mother's Day, my mom wanted to go back to Florida in order to visit my Dad's crypt. My husband, Michael, and I took her there. My brother, my sister-in-law, and their two kids also tagged along so we could all be together for Mother's Day. We had a nice dinner with all of my mom's friends in Florida. Every time my family goes to Florida, John Boy insists on going to Memory Gardens where my father is at rest, and Johnny says his prayers in Italian and Latin the way my mother taught him. And he tells his grandfather how much he loves him.

Now picture this: we are all at the table for dinner, with family and friends, and my husband says grace.

My mother started wiping her brow with a handkerchief before starting to eat. "Ugh, I am not feeling too well. Pretty soon I imagine I'll be seeing Gregory," which is my father.

All of a sudden Johnny Boy said to her, "How about Thursday, Grandma?" My mother didn't appreciate that, but everyone else had a good laugh.

In spite of this, Johnny was always close to my mother. The day came when my mother became ill and had to go to the hospital. Johnny was twenty-eight years old. Every day when he came home from his DayHab program, he would get ready to go to see his grandmother in the hospital. I would drive him, and he would sit beside the bed and tell his grandmother all about his day. He would tell her that she was going to get better, tell her how much he loved her, and he would pray in Italian with her. My mother looked forward to Johnny's visit every day.

About three weeks later, while Johnny was in his DayHab program, my mother passed away. That day when he came home he said, "Mom, I'm going to get ready to go to the hospital to see Grandma." With that, I grabbed hold of him and held him in my arms and hugged him.

"Johnny," I began, taking a deep breath, "Grandma is no longer with us. She passed away today."

He broke away from me and said very gently, "I am going up to my room."

I could hear him talking and praying in his room from my downstairs kitchen. I nervously sat around, occasionally dabbing my eyes with a tissue. After an hour, he came downstairs and walked over to me. He sat on the couch and clasped his hands together.

"Mom," he said solemnly, "even though Grandma died, life goes on, and she is with God."

I was blown away. *What a brave young man he is…and so connected with life.* He handled her wake and funeral better than I did.

My girlfriend Camille went to a psychic and is also a medium. As Camille sat down, the woman caressed her temple and said, "I cannot go on. There is this lady who *insists* you know a Johnny."

"Yes, he's my son, Pat's, best friend."

"Is he now? You tell Johnny that his grandmother is with him and is watching over him *all* the time."

When Camille came home, she called me and told me to give Johnny-Boy the message. While twirling my fork in the plate of spaghetti at dinner, I decided to relay this message and see if Johnny found it interesting.

"So, Johnny, Pat's mom went to a lady that can communicate with dead people."

"Oh yeah?" Johnny was chowing down on his dinner and didn't look up.

"Yeah, and do you know what she said?"

"What?"

"She said that Grandma told them that she is always watching over you all the time."

Now I had Johnny's attention. My Johnny looked at me seriously and told me, "Yes, Mom. I knew that. Grandma tells me that all the time."

I did not question him about it. I just let it be. Although, I wonder sometimes… I do know that Johnny is a gift from God. He is so very special.

Johnny the Charmer

Two years ago, John had to have his thyroid gland destroyed, as it was overactive and he was losing a lot of weight. The doctor advised us to have it destroyed, but it had to be done in the hospital. Johnny had to take a nuclear pill to do this.

"Now, Johnny," said the doctor, "you have to stay away from little children, infants, and pregnant women. Otherwise you could get them sick." Then he turned to me. "Mrs. Buttermark, this has to be done for three days. Because he has to stay away from these people, you might just consider keeping him at home for that time."

When he went back to the greenhouse after the three days, he saw Nancy Jones, who is staff member and who happens to be a grandmother. Nancy is well into her sixties.

"Nancy, don't come near me!"

"Why is that, Johnny?" Nancy looked bewildered.

So Johnny proceeded to tell Nancy, "You might be pregnant, and I could get you and your baby sick."

Nancy laughed and said, "Only you could say such a thing, John."

Recently John came home from working in the greenhouse with a beautiful bouquet of red roses. Many times he would come home with flowers for me or my daughter-in-law and her mother, Marianne. These flowers, however, were for my neighbor Rose.

Johnny told me, "I am going next door to give Rose her flowers." We assumed they came from the greenhouse, where he worked. Wrong. With that, the phone rang, and it was Rose. She told me that the roses were beautiful, and she started to laugh. She said that she asked Johnny where he got the beautiful roses.

Johnny's answer to her was, "At the funeral parlor. We pick them up and make beautiful bouquets out of them, and then we give them to nursing homes and to Meals on Wheels. The funeral parlors only throw them away, so we make good use of them."

We couldn't stop laughing.

Slacking Captain

Last July, our family went on a cruise to celebrate my granddaughter Caitlin's sixteenth birthday. We left New York on July 30 on the *Norwegian Jewel* for a trip to the Caribbean. There were seventeen of us, all family. Every night Johnny-Boy would put on his navy blue jacket, white pants, and of course his captain's hat. He would walk around the ship and everybody—and I mean everybody—would salute him.

One night as part of the entertainment on the ship, we went to an evening show. The theater was packed. The MC was on stage telling a few jokes. When he finished doing his thing, he told everyone in the audience, "Hey, whaddya know, the ship's captain is also in the audience." With that, a bright spotlight shone right on Johnny, who was sound asleep.

"Well, I sure hope the co-captain is steering the ship right now!" said the MC.

Everybody was laughing, which roused Johnny. He rubbed his eyes, stood up, turned around, and started saluting the audience.

Philanthropy

Johnny always went to 7-11. The store was only a few blocks from our home, so he would go, buy his candy, and come right back home. One day he went to get his candy alone and came back with a "friend."

Johnny flung open the door and said, "Mom! There's a man here."

Puzzled, I got up from the couch, where I sat beside John, and marched to the door. I gasped. There was a shaggy man with a crusty-looking, weathered brown jacket and torn up sneakers. He had a restless, almost crazy look in his eyes.

"Johnny, who is this?" I demanded.

"The man is hungry and asked me to please give him something to eat."

By this point, my husband also rose from the couch and stood protectively beside me. Thank God my husband was home.

"Just wait a second," I said, thinking it would be easier to make food than explain to Johnny what was going on. I hurriedly made the man a sandwich and sent him on his way. Johnny Boy looked satisfied, as if he just ate a Thanksgiving dinner, because he was happy that the man had some food. From that day on, Johnny was not allowed to go 7-11 anymore.

Epilogue

Reaping the Harvest

I've always believed in miracles. They were ever-present in my life—not only with Johnny's progress and his accomplishments. My father was once told he had inoperable cancer. He had such a strong faith in God that he wouldn't let it drag him down. In spite of his diagnosis, he lived for forty more years and ended up dying of a heart attack. Imagine that!

When raising John, life was difficult. I held strong to God and wanted him as a strong presence in Johnny's life also. Before we knew the specifics of Johnny's condition, we thought that maybe if he received Holy Communion and God's blessing, he would get better. I took him to the rectory of our church and asked to speak to one of the priests in charge. I waited in the rectory with Johnny-Boy, who was touching everything (and I was trying to stop him).

As Johnny lunged for the holy water and I flew after him, the priest walked in.

"Hello, there. What can I do for you today?"

He was tall, white-haired, and had ruddy cheeks, like he had been jogging outside. But he looked kind, and I had high hopes.

"Father, my son is not well. He's hyperactive, doesn't sleep, and I have to keep my eyes on him twenty-four-seven." I explained the situation in more detail, and the priest nodded, glancing at Johnny every so often.

"So I think it's important for Johnny to receive Holy Communion and God's blessing. I've been holding out hope for this, and it's very important for my husband and me."

The priest told me to sit down in the plush pew and sat beside me.

"Lucy, I know you want this and feel it's beneficial for John. But the problem is that it's not possible."

"Not possible? Why?" I sat stiffly beside him, moving over a few inches to look up at him in disbelief.

"John can't receive Holy Communion because he's incapable of understanding the true meaning of it."

"But Johnny is a child of God. He *should* be able to receive communion. Sure, he's special, but he's still a human being."

The priest shook his head and looked at me sadly. "It's just not possible. There's nothing I can do for you here."

That was enough for me. Without a word, I took my son by the hand and walked out of the rectory. I was devastated and angry. I knew that this was not the end of my quest for Johnny to receive Holy Communion… and I was right.

That incident soured me on the church, and I never had a connection with any of the priests in my area during the years I was raising Johnny. However, God works in mysterious ways. He knew that I needed someone like that in my life, and he sent a wonderful priest friend to our family. Msgr. Thomas P. Sandi came to our parish, and Peggy insisted that I meet him. After much back and forth, he came to visit Peggy and her family. I told her, "Okay, I'll give him a shot." And I met him. What a wonderful man he is and a true priest. I don't even consider him a monsignor; we go out with my daughter-in-law and girlfriends, and he's just like a close friend himself. He'd always tell me, "Lucy, you should really write a book about your experiences." I am so glad that he is in our lives and he has become part of our extended family.

When my husband and I celebrated our fiftieth wedding anniversary, Msgr. Sandi performed a renewal of our wedding vows. He made the ceremony so beautiful and so special. That's the way he is. He goes out of his way to make things special because he loves us. Currently he is pastor of Saint Elizabeth Anne Seton Church in Shrub Oak, New York. We still see him on a regular basis, as he visits us at least four times a year. Every time he comes to visit, he gives my Johnny-Boy a special blessing, which is all I've ever wanted.

As the years went on, Johnny continued to grow in faith, and everybody loves him. He has great manners, always smiles, and is a caring person. He is close to God and goes to church every Sunday. When mass is over, he holds the door until every one of the parishioners is out of the church. My husband and I just watch and smile. *What a gentleman!* He brings us so much joy. When God made Johnny, he threw away the mold.

My mother had taught Johnny how to pray in Italian. After all these years, he has never forgotten. He asks God every night to bless his family and everyone he knows. When someone is sick, people will call me on the phone and ask me to have Johnny pray for them. I hear him praying out loud in his bedroom, from his lips to God's ears, my special angel. Truly, I believe that John has a special connection with God and that God *does* answer his prayers. God has truly blessed me with this loving, truly good human being. If Johnny hears someone cursing or saying bad words, he says, "God, forgive them." We laugh, but really, it is a beautiful thing.

To this day, Johnny's leg is a problem. If he should bang it slightly or brush against something, the skin will open, as it is so sensitive there. I have to take him to the doctor to be treated. Even though this stops Johnny from going swimming, weight lifting, or going away with his peers, he still keeps a smile on his face and his great attitude. He accepts it. He finds fun by watching movies and enjoying superheroes. When the new Batman movie came out, you can bet that Johnny and Pat were there. Johnny saw it three times that opening weekend.

There are times in my life with Johnny that he breaks my heart, such as the time he asked me, "Why does my niece Briana have a car and I don't? I don't even drive," or, "Why is Michael, my brother, married and has children, and I don't?"

It is so sad. Johnny is so very aware of life. I hug him and tell him, "You are special, John, and God loves you more because you are his angel without wings."

John also grasps the reality about my husband's and my death. He asks, "What is going to happen to me when you and Dad grow older and die? Will I live here all alone?"

I reply, "You are so lucky you have a brother and sister-in-law who love you so much. They will see to it that you are taken care of."

I know in my heart that every mother and father who has a child with special needs wonders what will happen to their child when they grown up and they're not here. Who couldn't feel the pain and agony of that question? That is another burden these parents have. It is a heartache that never goes away. Thank God my son Michael and his wife, Peggy, will be there to take care of my son Johnny-Boy. That's why I am so blessed to have them.

Now Johnny is older, and I am reaping the harvest with him. I would not trade my life with him for the world, nor would I change a thing. I am so grateful and happy that God gave me Johnny-Boy.

Sometimes I ask people, "How old do you think I am?" Although people are taken aback, they are always shocked to hear my actual age.

"Nope, I'm much older than that," I say. "If you want to know my secret, it's my son. He keeps us young."

My son Michael is a better man for having a brother like John. My husband, John, also understands what life is about. *I* am a better person for having John. I just hope that when other parents read this book that they too will help their special needs children to reach their full potential in life and give them that chance. All they need is what my son Michael said: "Compassion, unconditional love, and patience." Please, parents, don't give up. If I did, Johnny-Boy would not have been the success story that I have written.

It's just as my father told me: "Nothing is impossible if you really want it, as long as it is something good." Throughout my years of trying to educate Johnny, trying to start a new school, and trying to make sure he'd not only live through his injury but also *thrive* through it, I clung to this phrase. Likewise, "Out of every tragedy, something good will come of it." Thanks to my father, no one knows the meaning of this phrase better than I do.

I mentioned I've always believed in miracles. That's because Johnny is living proof of their existence.

Thank You

My thanks and gratitude to the five sets of parents who were the founders of Eden II with me:

Mr. and Mrs. Joseph Casucci
Mr. and Mrs. Pat Mc Gowan
Mr. and Mrs. Arthur Potterfield
Mr. and Mrs. Jack Redmond
Mr. and Mrs. Anthony Vitsas

I would like to give a huge thanks to my son Michael; my daughter-in-law, Peggy; and my three granddaughters, Briana, Caitlin, and Lauren, who always said I could do this and gave me so much support and love.

I would like to give thanks to my friend Marianne Mezzacappa for helping me put this book together.

I would like to thank Anthony Ventrone for reinforcing the idea in my mind to write my story.

I would like to thank my friend Connie Monardo for helping me get on the right track.

A special thanks to all my dear friends—they know who they are.

I would like to thank my brother Gregory Perillo for being so positive and getting me excited about my book.

And last but not least, my husband, John, who never doubted me and was my backbone throughout this whole process. I love you!